INDUSTRY FRIENDS

INDUSTRY FRIENDS

CASEY DEXTER

NEW DEGREE PRESS

COPYRIGHT © 2022 CASEY DEXTER

INDUSTRY FRIENDS

ISBN   979-8-88504-061-7 *Paperback*
        979-8-88504-616-9 *Kindle Ebook*
        979-8-88504-166-9 *Ebook*

To my sister

CONTENTS

"In the midst of winter, I found there was, within me, an invincible summer."

—ALBERT CAMUS

AUTHOR'S NOTE

In my late twenties, I found myself on my first business trip to Scottsdale, Arizona. As I lay by the hotel pool, sipping a frozen cocktail and reading a magazine, I felt my muscles loosen, my jaw unclench, and the knot in my stomach unwind. I couldn't believe this was considered "business." For the first time in nearly two years, I was relaxed. As I closed the pages of my magazine, the woman on the cover caught my eye. I knew her. She used to be my boss.

I had achieved what I had considered to be my "dream job" by the age of twenty-five and quit just two short years later. The last thing I had quit was the cello in fourth grade. When my job didn't bring me the immeasurable amount of joy I'd expected, I felt betrayed. The podcasts, books, TV shows, and films I had once turned to for guidance and inspiration failed me. They all taught me how to work hard and pursue my passion, but none of them addressed what to do when I was dissatisfied. They didn't explain how I would know when it was time to leave. In fact, I noticed most stories stopped once the main character reached their goal. But what happens after? What if their goal wasn't what they expected?

In the pie chart of my life, I consider there to be five categories: career, family, love, friendships, and health. As hard as I try, the pieces never seem to be quite even. In my early twenties, those pieces fluctuated daily and I was obsessed with trying to find balance. I found I wasn't alone. My fellow twentysomethings were trying just as hard to establish themselves. Trying to make enough money. Trying to find their way in relationships, social circles, professional successes, hobbies, education, passions, fitness classes, spontaneous trips, Instagram fame, wardrobes, haircuts! Trying to be a caring son or daughter, a dependable brother or sister, an outgoing friend, a charismatic date, an intellectual student. Eager to carve their own paths, determined to prove their worth, and gaining and losing slivers of the "life pie" along the way.

While this novel is very fictional, I wanted the storyline of Olivia to feel believable. She's a twenty-five-year-old living in New York City, trying to make it all work. And it's killing her. She's so set on fulfilling one piece of her life that the rest begins to crumble around her. She's trying so hard in all the wrong places.

This book won't tell you how to get your dream job. And it won't tell you to quit your job either. But it will tell you that it's fine, expected even, for some pieces of the life pie chart to prevail while others are still baking. In fact, they will never all be even. I needed someone to tell me that. So this is Olivia telling you.

FALL

CHAPTER 1

Olivia had an eye for noticing details. The little ones often missed by the people around her.

She had this vision that when she died, God would neatly present her with a documented report of her lifetime observations. It'd chronicle the way she noticed her sister Gwen only dressed half her salad, how she spent more time in the TV studio than her home, how her stomach seemed to feel her emotions first. It'd show the rankings of the stickiest floors in the New York City bars she'd danced in with friends, and the ratings of all the boys she'd kissed over the years. She liked the idea that God had all these findings readily available upon her arrival to the pearly gates. That would be heaven.

As she walked down a busy Third Avenue, Olivia wondered where Scott would fall in the grand report of her life. Under the "boyfriends" chapter, she firmly decided, stopping in front of an East Village coffee shop. Sure, they weren't necessarily "together," but that was about to change.

She took a deep breath and pulled on the oversized door handle. As if an internal compass had been activated, Olivia's gaze immediately fell upon Scott.

The sun beamed onto his face from the windows. It perfectly illuminated his ash brown hair, highlighted his chiseled jawline, and made his green eyes smolder and shine. If Scott didn't work in sales, Olivia would have been convinced he'd set up this perfect shot the way the camera crew did in rehearsals. She imagined the tech guys seating Scott at the table, playing with the blinds, scooting the chair back, holding a bounce card to catch the glimmer in his pupils. "We got the shot!" they'd announce excitedly. "He looks like a real heartbreaker!" the director would muse.

Olivia thought back to the taxi where they first kissed, the park where they mixed mimosas in water bottles, the H&M in Soho where she picked out shirts for him.

Scott looked up and gave a soft smile. She felt her stomach somersault. Olivia took another deep inhale. *Ready … action!* she thought to herself.

She tossed her long brown hair over her shoulder, adjusted her leather jacket, and walked toward her soon-to-be-boyfriend. This was it. Scott was *finally* going to ask her to be his girlfriend. They'd been seeing each other for several months now, practically ever since he joined her friend group by way of Luke, her friend from college.

Maybe after she said yes, they'd spend the rest of the day walking through Washington Square Park, holding hands and soaking up the last few sunny days of October. Or they'd take the L train to Brooklyn and sit at a brewery, laughing as she tried to count all the freckles on his face. She'd purposefully worn her leather jacket because she knew it made her look cool and effortless, gold hoop earrings because Scott had complimented them once, and a low-cut top because she was a girl and Scott was a boy and whatever.

Scott's emerald eyes looked into hers as she sat down across from him. "They have a chai tea latte on the menu." He smirked. "That's redundant, chai *is* tea."

She set her bag on the chair and giggled. "You should tell the manager!"

"Or maybe Violet James!" he exclaimed. "Maybe she can do a story about it." He spread out his hands, miming a headline. "Special report, coffee shops across the country use improper name!"

"Violet *Jones*," Olivia corrected warmly. She tucked her hair behind her ear. "Her name is Violet Jones. You know, The Happiest TV Host in America?" she quipped, reciting the show's tagline.

"Right, right." Scott waved his hand through the air. "I always forget." She caught a whiff of his familiar cologne. Earthy, musky, and fresh. *So dreamy*, she thought. "Well, thanks for meeting me," he continued, sliding his chair closer to the table. Olivia felt her pulse quicken. Any second now. *Cue: The Ask.*

Olivia pulled on a strand of hair. She tried to catch his gaze, but he kept looking away. Was he nervous?

Scott finally cleared his throat, "So." He looked down at his hands. "I—I don't think I can be who you want me to be."

Olivia's smile froze. "Oh?"

He wiped the corners of his mouth. "I don't think I can, you know," he gestured to her, "do this anymore." He let out a sigh and dropped his hands in his lap.

The smile on Olivia's face vanished. The coffee shop exploded. The mugs, saucers, tiny plates with croissants, smashed on the floors and ricocheted off the walls. The kettle whistled loudly and steam filled the back bar. Coffee beans scattered across the entryway, patrons slipped left and right. She squeezed her eyes shut. The world was spinning.

"Olivia?"

She blinked. "You don't want to be together?" she asked weakly.

Scott cast his eyes downward and shook his head. "My ex really messed me up. I'm just not ready for this. Sorry, Liv."

His ex-girlfriend from *three* years ago? Olivia wasn't expecting this. She was unprepared.

"Wh—what are we going to tell our friends?" she stammered.

"What is there to tell them?" he asked bluntly. "That we're not dating?"

The coffee shop suffered another small earthquake as Scott spoke. Tea bags slid off their rows on the shelves. Whipped cream and sauce toppings shot like darts. The brown liquid in Scott's mug splashed onto the table, burning into the wood like acid. To-go lattes flew into the glass windows, hitting with a thud before sliding down to reveal frothy skid marks.

It was all Olivia could do but make a small nod. It was over. She wished she'd ordered a cup of coffee so she could throw it in Scott's face.

When she'd first met Scott, Olivia had described him to Gwen as Grand Central Station. Of course everyone knew it as the popular New York City train station, but there was so much inside. A food market, a hidden speakeasy, tennis courts! As she got to know Scott more and more, she discovered something new every week and it enticed her. She loved a challenge. It made her feel like she understood him better than any of her other friends.

Her eyes darted nervously around the coffee shop: a man on his computer, two women staring at their phones in the corner, a young girl photographing her cappuccino. What was Olivia supposed to do now, leave? She cleared her throat.

"So, what have we been doing for the past four months?" she said low and tersely.

Scott pushed his mug away. "I don't know. Just hanging?"

"Hanging?" she croaked.

They'd gone to concerts, played tennis, made homemade pizza, Scott dabbing the tip of her nose with flour. He'd even coaxed her into attending a baseball game with him. She hated the Yankees! To demote all of that to "hanging" felt like calling a home run a strike.

Scott sighed and ran his hand through his effortlessly styled hair. "Look, it's more than that. I just feel like you have your whole life planned out. You're too obsessed with work."

Flashes of her and Scott and the future life she'd imagined for them ran through her mind. The scenes she envisioned just before falling asleep at night: the two of them visiting the Rockefeller Christmas tree, attending swanky company parties on the Upper East Side, renting a beach house in the Hamptons for all their friends and family every Labor Day, Olivia laughing loudly as Scott donned an apron and attempted to boil a lobster. Him on her arm as she walked the red carpet at the Emmys, then crying as she thanked him in her acceptance speech and told their kids watching at home "to go to bed!" Violet Jones had this life, why couldn't Olivia?

She quickly blinked her eyes. "I didn't realize you f—felt that way," Olivia stammered. Sure she had to cancel dates here and there because of breaking news or an urgent ask from her manager, Andrea, but she thought he'd understood.

Scott continued running his hand through his hair. Olivia wished he would stop. "You work all the time. All for what, to become a TV producer?" he questioned.

Now Scott sounded like her mother.

"What's so wrong with knowing what I want?" she retorted. She could feel her cheeks getting hot. "I love television."

The hours were long, and the pay was low and sometimes all she could afford for dinner was frozen mac and cheese from Duane Reade, but it was all part of her plan. That's showbiz! It would all pay off one day.

"Well, I'm just looking for fun right now," he stated.

Olivia wondered where all of this was suddenly coming from. She raised an eyebrow and crossed her arms. "You seemed to have fun when my job got you and Luke those Drake tickets for free," she accused tartly.

Now it was Scott's cheeks who grew red. "Drake's my man!" He rubbed his jaw, his fingers fidgeting. "I wasn't gonna miss that!"

Olivia rolled her eyes and leaned back in her chair.

"I don't get it," she murmured. "You don't want to be successful and live in New York City?"

He shook his head. "It's not that." He dropped his hands from his face and reached for his mug. His fingers slowly began tracing the ceramic rim.

"Then what is it?" Her voice quavered.

Olivia watched as his fingers made tiny circles again and again until they abruptly stopped. Scott dropped his hands in his lap and looked up at her.

"I just don't want those things," he swallowed, "with you."

The final earthquake caused the entire coffeeshop to cave in. The roof, the walls, all collapsed in a pile of smoking debris. There was nothing but rubble around them. It was all gone.

She thought she'd done everything right. Made special dinner reservations, played his favorite music, adjusted her schedule to fit his as best as she could. Of course, work came first, and she still made time for Gwen and her best friend, Margot. But she thought she was making it all work. It hadn't exactly been easy.

"Well then," choked Olivia. "It doesn't seem like there's anything else to discuss."

She stood and grabbed her bag off the chair and slung it over her shoulder. She tucked her long hair behind her ear.

"Don't say that, Liv." Scott reached his arm out across the table and touched her wrist. "We're friends. I care about you. I can't explain it. I just can't right now."

He stared up at her from the table. The sun had stopped shining on his face. His skin was no longer illuminated, the twinkle in his eyes was lost. His hair—well, his hair was still perfect—but the scene was trashed. The act was over. It seemed like flawless lighting was just for television, not real life. Their relationship, not-relationship, whatever it was called, was cut. There was nothing more to play out.

"I have to go," she whispered, willing herself not to cry.

Olivia readjusted her bag and zipped her jacket all the way up to her chin. How dare he not want to date someone that tried so hard for him.

"We'll always be friends," he offered, looking less distressed than Olivia cared to see.

Friends?

Olivia turned her feet toward the door and tried to think of a farewell line that would sting, that would haunt him late at night, that would make him regret this decision.

"Well, I guess I'll see you around," she offered. *Ah, that definitely wasn't it.*

CHAPTER 2

An alarm clock rang in the small bedroom that held light-colored furniture and a single hanging rack in the corner. The bed wasn't far from the door, which wasn't far from the window, which could hardly be called a window considering it didn't open all the way and only let in a very tiny sliver of light. No light shone through now as Olivia silenced the alarm and reached for her phone. It was 3:45 a.m.

I will not think about Scott, she thought as she squeezed her eyes tight and yawned. *I will not think about Scott.*

She switched on the only lamp in the room before walking down the hallway to the bathroom, not bothering to avoid the one squeaky floorboard since Gwen was away on business. She hated when her sister left her alone in their apartment.

Shortly after, Olivia returned to her room and dressed herself in a brown skirt, ankle boots with a comfortable heel, and a long-sleeved black sweater. She added curls to her hair and makeup to her olive skin and dark eyes and called a car through an app on her phone (the one company-covered perk of having to be in the studio so early).

The mornings at work were already busy without Scott on her mind. She'd have to wait until the show was over until she could replay yesterday's conversation in her mind.

As if she hadn't done so already a hundred times last night as she fell asleep...

No matter what was happening in her life—like the time the ceiling leaked directly above her bed, or when she dropped her wallet down the narrow gap between the platform and the subway, or the dinner date she spent with a guy who repeatedly told her she was funny "for a girl"— there was always one thing Olivia could count on: *America's Happy Hour.*

Airing live at 8:00 a.m. eastern, five days a week, *Happy Hour* hit the airwaves to the delight of its targeted 25 to 54 aged demographic. Covering everything from small-town heroes to international breaking news to new work-outs proven to break a sweat to sweaters for the fall, *Happy Hour* was consistently Atlas Broadcast Group's highest-rated morning show.

Atlas' impressive skyscraper was still cloaked in darkness when Olivia arrived. It was impossible to see its true height as the night surrounded its glassy edifice. The building was mysterious, enigmatic. It reflected the edge, the coolness and confidence of those who ran the megahit shows inside. It was exactly where Olivia always dreamed she'd be.

The few staffers in the dimly lit third floor office didn't look up from their computers as Olivia entered. She smiled anyway on the off chance one of them greeted her. They'd eventually address her if they needed a script changed or a run to the props department.

Olivia set her bag down at the last seat on the end of a row of gray desks. She turned on her computer and watched her inbox quickly fill with emails ending in:

"ASAP."

She double clicked a server called "Rundown." As a production assistant, the lowest on the staff totem pole, it was her job to manage the database that housed the show's scripts, graphics, videos, and promos. The rundown acted as a digital bible every morning for all crew, producers, directors, and talent to reference for up-to-date information on the show as they readied for air.

To the outside eye, it would look like a set of abbreviations punctured by undefined symbols and segment titles, but to Olivia it was a second language in which she was fluent. She loved the intricacies of formatting, the detail to organization and flow. The hours she'd spent learning to code on MySpace as a teen had somehow paid off. She knew her manager, Andrea, would never say it, but Olivia was good at her job. The rundown was always perfect.

Olivia clicked between the server's folders, checking the photos inside and rapidly printing the scripts for each segment. It was crucial to focus on these elements. A mistake here would affect the show on air. She could *not* think about Scott right now. She also didn't want to cry in the office.

After forty-five minutes of intense scrutiny, she rose from her chair, collected the scripts from the printer, and wrapped a rubber band around a set of five thick notecards. She then headed to the large elevator bank that would take her down to the studio.

The first bright light Olivia saw all morning came from the honey-hued LED screens and studio spotlights. With golden undertones and jewel-colored furniture, the studio felt like a living room in a very expensive northeast contemporary home. The large, rectangular ivory rug lay in the center underneath a striking white marble desk.

Olivia's boots lightly thudded against the shiny studio floors as she weaved her way through the giant set cameras. Violet Jones' desk was wide, oval shaped and on wheels, making it easy to roll away for cooking segments and Judo demonstrations alike. She felt the heat from the powerful studio lights on her back as she laid down the five notecards, one pink highlighter, and one blue Signo ballpoint pen on the smooth surface. Printed using size 16 font, .5 margins, and with no more than five bullet points, every notecard held facts, figures, and interview questions for Violet determined by her producers. Just before the show, Violet would grab the notecards and use the highlighter and pen combo to make her own notes in the margin. It's where she thought of additional questions and the zinging one-liners she was famous for: *"A tip for you and a sip for me!"* *"Grab the wine for this headline!"* If the notecards were off, Violet was off.

"What was the point of all of those AP classes if you're just a glorified Kinkos?" Olivia's mom once asked during Christmas dinner as Olivia explained the role to the family.

Olivia stabbed her fork into her potatoes. They'd gone over this before. "This is what everyone has to do in order to become a producer. It's just the way it is."

"But you're overqualified!" stressed her mom.

"Actually, Mom," chimed Gwen, looking up from her plate of vegetables. "It's statistically harder to get Olivia's job than to get into Harvard. She beat out like three hundred other candidates." Gwen patted Olivia's shoulder reassuringly.

Her mother raised her eyebrows in what Olivia could only deem as her mom's signature move. "Well you never got coffee for anyone, Gwen." she stated very matter-of-factly.

"She also never met Will Ferrell!" Olivia interjected. *"And made him laugh."* Technically it was her coworker Hallie who'd made Will laugh, but Olivia was still there.

Olivia shook the memory from her mind and waved to the camera operators, audio techs, stagehands, and Sal, the stage manager. They all returned her wave in earnest. At least the crew was friendly. She turned and walked back to the elevator bank.

Several more times throughout the morning she made her way back and forth to the studio, delivering scripts, dropping off coffees, checking the hair and makeup schedules, and answering her phone in an increasingly rushed manner. At the end of every task, she returned to more and more emails in her inbox.

"Can you find this photo? Ken needs coffee. Changes in the closing script. Update the rundown! Did you find that photo? Need it NOW."

She took a deep breath in and slowly let it out. It would all get done. It always did. The staff counted on her to meet their requests, and while it wasn't always glamorous, it felt good to be needed. Contributing to the show's success was the only way she'd climb the ranks.

As the morning neared eight o'clock, Olivia brought a final script change down to the studio. She felt a blister forming on her heel as she stepped into the elevator and cursed herself for not wearing thicker socks. She was tragically behind on laundry.

Since she was nose deep in the script pages, it wasn't until the announcement of her floor that she looked up and saw the man standing next to her was Jake Gyllenhaal. She gave a shy smile and tucked her hair behind her ear.

"Have a good one!" He beamed as the doors opened.

"Have a good one!" She repeated like a parrot. Olivia really needed to work on her exit lines with men.

Celebrity sightings in the morning were so normal that she was rarely caught off guard: Steven Spielberg, Steph Curry, Oprah, the cast of *Jersey Shore* (who were surprisingly tanner in person). When Olivia had first started a year and a half ago, it was all she could do but muster a weak smile in return without her knees buckling.

Olivia moved briskly through the hallway, trying not to favor her throbbing ankle. She passed by the small catering kitchen and saw a flash of blonde hair.

"Hallie!" Olivia beamed as she greeted her friend. Hallie's wide blue eyes twinkled as she stepped into the hallway. "Look at that jacket!" Olivia continued, admiring her friend's pink fitted blazer.

Hallie gave an excited wave. "Thanks, Liv! Violet gave it to me," she explained as she touched the satin sleeves. "She said she didn't want it anymore." Hallie shrugged.

"Lucky you! It looks really great," replied Olivia as she studied the silky material, the shiny lapel. With small pink buttons and narrow zippers on the pockets, it looked expensive and powerful. Olivia remembered Violet wearing it in one of her first shows.

"Runway Mondays," announced Olivia, putting on her best anchor voice.

"Looks you'll love…" chimed Hallie, acting as her coanchor.

"For less!" they said in unison.

Hallie did a spin and strutted as if she were going down a catwalk. Olivia laughed and followed behind her down the hallway.

They continued walking together, passing the green rooms, the hair and makeup stations, the props department. Photos lined the walls, displaying pictures from Atlas' past shows. Black and white memories of former hosts and programs that had filmed in the studio, that had used these same rooms in preparation.

"I have gossip for you," whispered Hallie as they arrived at the first door to Violet's dressing room. The room was so large it had two entrances. Olivia's eyes widened.

As Violet's assistant, Hallie always had the best gossip. Her proximity to Violet, coupled with her easygoing, nonthreatening demeanor allowed her to overhear many private conversations.

Hallie twisted the doorknob. "She's not in here," she explained quickly. "She's doing a run-through on set." They slipped inside; Hallie gently closed the door behind them. Olivia placed the new script on Violet's desk and looked expectantly at Hallie.

"Wesley got promoted," she revealed.

Olivia's eyes flashed. "How do you know?"

"I overheard Andrea this morning." Hallie grinned. She walked around the dressing room, fluffing pillows and throwing away Violet's lipstick-stained napkins.

Olivia bounced on her toes. "So there's an open associate producer role now?" The timing couldn't be more perfect. She tapped her fingers against her skirt. "I'm not really close with Wesley or else I'd ask."

"I know, same," said Hallie. "He's always in the edit rooms." She moved a vase of flowers from one table to another. "Maybe ask Andrea?"

Olivia pictured herself receiving a promotion. Moving up the ladder faster than any other production assistant in

Happy Hour history. Violet would look past Andrea in pitch meetings and say directly, "What do you think, Olivia?" They'd become best friends, confidants. Traveling in private jets across the world, interviewing political leaders and activists and *American Idol* winners. Violet would insist on giving Olivia her own seat behind the white marble desk. "People need to hear what you have to say, Liv!" The world would know her name. *Take that, Scott!*

"Yeah." She smiled at Hallie. "I think I will."

Olivia glanced at the clock on her phone. 7:45 a.m. "I have to head to the Control Room," she announced.

Hallie nodded and they exited Violet's dressing room together. Olivia eyed the interns' desk just across the hallway, next to the studio doors. Two young girls were seated, sipping enormous frappuccinos with whip and caramel toppings.

"How much are the interns getting paid these days?" she whispered into Hallie's ear. Olivia knew with her own thirteen-dollars-an-hour paycheck, she couldn't afford many coffees like those.

Hallie laughed and rolled her eyes. "The interns get a coffee stipend now. It's new," she whispered back as they continued walking.

"You're kidding," Olivia choked. Hallie shook her head. "I barely get paid enough to afford water! I bet they complained to their executive dads."

"Probably," responded Hallie, who was the daughter of a single mother and thought dads caused most of the world's issues anyway.

"You get all the good gossip down here," noted Olivia as she changed the subject. They were almost outside the Control Room now. "And all the good clothes! Do you think Andrea would give me one of *her* old jackets?"

Hallie snorted. "I do *not* think you want one of Andrea's jackets. It's probably covered in cat hair."

Olivia covered her mouth to stifle her laughter as they arrived at the door. "See you after the show," Hallie continued. "I want to hear about your weekend!"

Olivia felt a knot in her stomach as she reached for the handle. She didn't want to talk about Scott, let alone the heartache that happened on Sunday. *The Heartache That Happened on Sunday*. It sounded like the name of a band or a new bar in the West Village.

The door opened and Olivia nearly collided with a stocky, thin-haired man.

"Watch where you're going!" he exclaimed. "I'm late to greet Denzel!"

An overwhelming wave of cigarette smoke surrounded her. "Sorry, Smith. Excuse me," said Olivia. He waved his clipboard dramatically and walked away in a huff.

Fifteen massive screens filled the front wall of the Control Room, each showing different variations of the glossy studio. Three rows of computers lined the floors, with staffers wearing headsets and speaking in code. "We only have a minute-forty for the close!" "Legal says she has to read the full statement!" This room was the real heartbeat of the show. Everything that happened here dictated what viewers saw on their TVs. Olivia's presence was to ensure the rundown was correct should any changes or breaking news happen on the fly. For live television, that was pretty often.

Olivia took her seat in the front row of computers next to a woman in a mustard yellow sweater.

"Good morning, Andrea." Olivia smiled as she set down her notebook.

Andrea grunted and turned to face the row directly behind her.

"Taped pieces look clean, Ken," she barked. "We're cleared to do the story on that family who lives by the tainted water." Her thick New Jersey accent ate up the words "family" and "water." *Fahm-ly. Wudder.*

"Excellent," replied a tall, bean-pole man with faded red hair and expensive glasses.

"Pete, is the crew set?" Andrea called again, adjusting her sweater as she turned directly to her right.

"Crew's set," the bearded man responded. "Five minutes to air." He adjusted his microphone.

Olivia clicked into the rundown, double checking every video and graphic that would be used during air. She read through the intro scripts and made sure they were listed under the tab labeled "teleprompter." The room was abuzz as everyone else made their final checks, the clock ticking down.

"Alright gang, going live in ten ... nine ..." announced Pete.

"Let's have a good show, everyone!" boomed Ken, who, even seated, still towered over most of the staff. From the time of her first interview, Olivia always thought Ken resembled a gawky, more aloof Conan O'Brien. Tragically, Ken was just as funny as Andrea was kindhearted. Still, as the show's executive producer, Olivia trusted Ken as a seasoned expert.

"Eight ... seven, slide the music in!" thundered Pete.

Olivia scooted her chair closer to the computer. She looked up at the giant screens and saw the notecards perfectly aligned on the anchor desk. If she squinted, she could almost see pink-highlighted lines. Violet sat behind the desk in an all-white suit, her short black hair falling perfectly above her shoulders. Her lipstick was bright red and powerful against her dark brown skin. Violet had a way of pulling off intensity while still showing wit and compassion. It was why thousands of viewers tuned in every day.

"Looking great, Violet!" mused Andrea into her mouthpiece.

"Six ... five ... four!" continued Pete. The theme song grew louder over his voice.

Olivia's skin prickled. No matter how many times she heard the countdown to air, the preshow jitters never went away. It was one of the things she loved most about live television. It was so present. It would be impossible to think about Scott at a time like this.

"Rolling!" announced Pete. "Ready camera one. Take camera one!" He animatedly flung his arms in the air as if he were conducting the cameras in a symphony. "Three ... two ... one! We're live!"

CHAPTER 3

At precisely 9:01 a.m., the show was off the air and the staff began to clear out of the Control Room. Olivia met Hallie in the catering kitchen where they made large instant coffees and carried them back up to the office. The thirty-minute grace period between the end of the day's show and the prep for tomorrow's was the only down time they had each morning.

Hallie sat next to Olivia, sipping her coffee as she watched her friend scroll through the job openings on the Atlas Careers page. She excitedly nudged Olivia's shoulder when they saw *Happy Hour: Associate Producer* newly listed at the top.

Olivia could hear Scott's voice saying, *"All for what, to become a TV producer?"* She quickly hit "Apply."

The rest of the day was spent compiling research, logging footage, transcribing videos, and prepping the rundown for Tuesday's show. The sun had begun its descent by the time Olivia started her walk home.

She texted Gwen:

"Sushi for dinner?"

Gwen answered:

"Yes, my flight just got in. I'll meet you there."

Olivia let out a sigh of relief, grateful she'd have her sister back. Gwen had a way of easing Olivia's anxiety. An incoming call appeared on the screen. Olivia felt her muscles tense as she moved the phone to her ear, running the last few steps across Madison Avenue to avoid a speeding taxi.

"Olivia, where are you?" questioned her mother. "It's so loud."

Olivia skirted around a group of tourists. "Sorry, it's rush hour. I'm just heading home now." She sucked in a breath of air and let it out slowly as she continued walking.

"That's a long day," contemplated her mom. "More than twelve hours."

"Yep, I know," replied Olivia, pursing her lips. A SUV honked its horn. A second SUV honked its horn at the first SUV. A biker dinged his bell.

"Did you have a good weekend?" her mother asked.

"Uh, yeah," she said, shifting her phone to her left ear, careful to avoid stepping in dog poop. A man tried to hand her a flyer. She shook her head. "I went to a concert with Margot. The Jonas Brothers. They were on the show last week so I got free tickets to their performance. It was cool actually because—"

"That's great." Her mom's voice sounded muffled, farther from the receiver. Olivia could hear noises in the background. "Just press restart, Robert!"

Olivia walked by a street vendor selling designer purses. She pressed the phone closer to her ear. "Mom?"

Her mom's voice returned. "Your father is having issues with his computer," she explained.

Olivia turned onto a quieter side street. "Mom, I'm meeting Gwen for dinner soon, so I have to go." She could picture her parents hunched over their country-style kitchen table, staring at her dad's laptop with confusion. She didn't feel like hearing about how it was "the computer's fault."

"Already?" her mother asked. "OK. Bye honey."

Olivia dropped her phone in her bag and continued the ten blocks to the restaurant.

She spotted Gwen in their usual booth. Two glasses of red wine and an order of edamame sat on the table. The place wasn't fancy and they were the youngest among the early dinner crowd, but that's why they liked it. The sushi was fresh and the atmosphere was quiet. It was a nice setting to talk about their careers, family, boyfriends, not-boyfriends, and reflect on life in general. The girls discovered it when they'd first moved in together two years ago and it quickly became a ritual whenever they needed a good catching up. Even though they lived together and were only two years apart in age, the sisters lived vastly different lives.

"Good call with the wine," remarked Olivia as she sat down. "How was your trip? I transferred you my half of the rent by the way," she added. There was now $201.56 in her bank account until her next paycheck. She secretly hoped Gwen would pick up the tab for dinner.

"Thanks," Gwen said, nodding. She brushed her brown hair out of her eyes. It was just a little shorter than Olivia's. And Gwen was just a little taller and just a little thinner than her sister. "The conference was amazing!" she answered. Olivia crunched down on edamame and nodded approvingly. "I mean, it was just me and a bunch of old guys. You know, senior tech executives, but it was good for visibility."

To the joy of their parents, Gwen was the youngest manager to date at her financial technology company. "Fintech," as everyone with an Apple Watch referred to it. Olivia really wasn't sure what Gwen did, but she knew her sister traveled often, led a team of analysts, some who were older and had families of their own, and frequently won awards for her outstanding presentations and campaigns.

"That's great." Olivia smiled. She noticed Gwen hadn't touched her drink and wondered if she was on another health kick. Gwen's boney collarbone peeked out from her thick camel-colored sweater.

"I'm glad you wanted to get dinner," said Gwen. "Look," she tapped her fingers nervously on the table. Olivia noticed her pink nail polish was mostly picked off. "There's something I need to tell you," she continued. She spoke softly, diplomatically, like she was in a meeting with one of her account managers.

"There's something I need to tell you, too," replied Olivia, thinking back to Sunday. "But you go first."

"No, you," Gwen insisted.

They both hesitated.

"Scott and I—"

"I got the London offer."

"What?" exclaimed Olivia. "Y—you got the—?"

"I got the offer," repeated Gwen. Her face was stuck between excitement and terror. "To work in London. I'd run the whole division."

A bottle of soy sauce hit the wall, breaking into a hundred pieces. Spicy tuna, rice, and avocado exploded from the kitchen, coating the ceiling and the hair of the woman in the booth behind them. The edamame came to life and dove off the table like synchronized swimmers into the pool of miso soup flooding the floors below. The liquid quickly rose higher and higher, surely they would all drown!

Olivia reopened her eyes. *How many times can the world end in one week?*

A waitress Olivia didn't recognize placed a tray of sushi between them. "Enjoy!" she smiled. "Hey, are you two twins?"

"No, just sisters," said Gwen quietly, smoothing the napkin on her lap.

It was a warm October evening, but Olivia suddenly felt very cold. She hugged her elbows. "You're moving?" She gulped.

Gwen nodded solemnly. "Gavin said there's an opening in the London office. It's a huge promotion," she explained. "If I don't take it now, it'll be gone."

Olivia read the expression on Gwen's face. It was the same hardened look she made whenever she worked out, or called their landlord, or found Olivia's dirty dishes still in the sink. Her eyebrows furrowed, lips pressed firmly together. She was serious.

"You're leaving New York City?" repeated Olivia.

"Yes," said Gwen. Her face softened. The corners of her mouth turned down. "In about a month."

"A month!" Olivia choked. "Wow, that's really soon." She looked around the restaurant, wishing someone would drop a plate or spill their glass, anything to cause a commotion and delay this conversation.

"You knew this was a possibility, Liv," reasoned Gwen lightly. "I've said I've wanted to go to London for a while now, it's the heartbeat of the company!"

Olivia nodded and took a sip of water. She stared at their untouched sushi rolls until they morphed and blended together. *Why does everything good have to end? First Scott, now Gwen.* She was just starting to feel really settled, secured in New York. It wasn't fair.

"I'm sorry Livvy, I really am," consoled Gwen. She grabbed her sister's arm across the table. "I would have told you sooner if I'd known. But of course, I didn't even want to tell you now." She rubbed Olivia's arm soothingly. "Also, Scott? Did something happen?"

Olivia's heart sat somewhere in her stomach. Her hunger was gone. A heavy ache filled her limbs. "Can we go home?" she croaked, craving the comfort and privacy of their apartment.

"Yes, of course." Gwen waved over the waitress and asked for a box and the check. She slid into the booth next to Olivia and wrapped her arm around her. "Oh, I'm so sorry, Liv. Are you mad at me?"

Olivia shook her head and took a deep breath. "No. I've just never lived in New York without you," she sniffed. Two tears rolled down her cheeks. One for Gwen and one for Scott.

CHAPTER 4

Olivia had eyed Andrea's office door all week. Like a rat scouring for pizza on the subway tracks: jittery, on edge, aware that mere seconds stood between success and defeat.

Openings seemed to fill quickly, and Olivia knew it was important to speak to Andrea early about becoming an associate producer. She wanted to show Andrea she was serious. Unfortunately, Andrea's office door remained closed most of the week; she never let anyone inside. Olivia imagined it was like a cave, with Andrea only ever emerging from its depths to speak to Ken or a producer.

The week had flown by with a steady stream of breaking news. Olivia hadn't made it home even one night before six o'clock, leaving little time for her to run errands, work out, or soak in her last month with Gwen before going to bed at eight thirty and doing it all again. By Friday, she was exhausted.

At 4:56 p.m., she said goodbye to Hallie and watched her leave the office in her pink jacket just as Andrea was coming back from the bathroom. Olivia's eyes lit up as she quickly hopped out of her chair. "Andrea! Do you have a second?"

"Not really," replied Andrea tersely. She wore a green wool sweater, baggy slacks, and black boots. She wasn't old, and she wasn't ugly, but she put herself together as if she didn't want people looking at her. She hardly wore makeup, seldom a fitted article of clothing, and kept her mousy brown hair in a sensible, low-maintenance bun.

Olivia realized this may be her only chance. "Sorry, I know you're super busy. It's just—" She had to hustle to keep up with Andrea's pace. "I saw the opening for the associate producer role, and I was interested so—"

"HR deals with position openings," grunted Andrea as she neared her office door. Olivia saw her window of opportunity was closing.

"Right," she nodded eagerly, "I was hoping to talk to you about it. You know, as my manager," continued Olivia, "who I look up to and—" Maybe flattery could buy her some more time?

Andrea turned and faced Olivia. "If you want to be an associate producer, go help Smith with his bread-less bread segment."

"Is that a thing?" Olivia blurted.

Andrea eyed Olivia's turtleneck dress with the face of a disapproving school principal. Olivia suddenly felt very self-conscious. It was a modest outfit, chic even, but Andrea's silent judgment made her take a small step back.

"Um, great," continued Olivia. "That would be great, thanks." She glanced at the big clock on the office wall. What was another forty-five minutes?

Andrea strode into her office and sat down at her desk. Without looking up she said, "Think of Smith as a mentor." She switched on her lamp. "Close the door behind you."

Olivia pulled the glass door shut and looked over at Smith, who was nose-to-screen at his desk. Tonight she had RSVP'd yes to Lucy's birthday party, but staying a bit later couldn't hurt. She wanted to show Andrea she was serious. And if that meant helping Smith, then that's what she'd do.

~

Forty-five minutes turned into two hours, and Olivia learned "mentorship" just meant Smith criticizing every photo and B-roll clip she selected. "B-roll is supporting video! It should provide context to the segment, not just more imagery of bread!" he had commanded. Still, Olivia looked forward to watching Andrea's reaction in the control room next week. She really hoped she'd be proud.

With a deep yawn, she raced home, straightened her long dark hair, put on her favorite knee-high leather boots, and helped herself to a tight, long-sleeved black dress from Gwen's closet. If Gwen had been home, she would've let Olivia borrow it. Probably.

Olivia considered canceling, longing for a blissful snooze on her couch, but knew she couldn't do that to Lucy, a close friend from college who was dating her other good friend, Luke. The same Luke who had introduced Olivia to Scott. It was a twisted web and another reason why Olivia knew she had to attend tonight's party. She'd noticed Scott had RSVP'd "No" and wanted to take advantage of a night out without him.

The music from the bar could be heard from the street. Olivia saw Margot's light brown hair through the window and let out a deep breath she didn't realize she was holding. In the same way she felt comforted when she came home to Gwen in their apartment, it was a sigh of relief. The satisfaction of knowing she was no longer alone and had someone she trusted around her. Margot was practically family. As Gwen would say, "She's one of us." It's how they referred to friends that they knew fit into their sister bond.

"Livvy!" Margot threw her arms in the air as soon as Olivia's boots crossed the threshold. Margot and Olivia had been inseparable since freshman year of college. Olivia couldn't imagine New York without her. *She'll probably move to London, too.* She'd yet to tell Margot the news about Gwen. Saying it out loud to her meant that it was all real. That Gwen was really leaving. She hated that.

"You look hot!" Margot hollered, pulling Olivia into a hug. That was another thing Olivia loved about Margot. She wasn't afraid to be loud, to take up space. Olivia had a feeling Margot acted exactly the same in public exactly as she did when she was home alone. Completely unabashed.

For a body of mostly limbs that slightly resembled that of a teenage boy who'd just experienced a growth spurt, the hug was surprisingly comforting and warm.

"He's a dipshit!" Margot fumed. "An idiot!" A few people in the bar turned around, Margot didn't seem to notice.

"I'm okay, it's fine," lied Olivia, uncomfortable with the stares. She gestured for Margot to sit at the empty table just beside them. Lucy had yet to arrive.

"Let me just say this once so we can move on and enjoy the night." Margot adjusted her hoop earring and leaned closer to Olivia, careful to avoid the industrial lamp that hung low in between them. "Dating Scott would've been a nightmare. The quicker you can move on the better!"

Olivia nodded. She wasn't a fan of tough love. She preferred to be coddled. Who didn't? But that wasn't Margot's style. Besides, Margot had a good radar as a seasoned dater in the city. Bankers, athletes, agents, the guy who drove the Zamboni at Rangers games, she'd seen it all.

"I mean it," continued Margot, scooting her metal chair in closer. "If there was a word stronger than nightmare I'd go with that."

"Hell? Inferno?" Olivia guessed. "Comm 220?"

Margot raised an eyebrow at the mention of the worst class they'd ever taken together. She pinched her nose and deepened her voice, "With Professor Jeremy Larkin?" She kept her nose scrunched and hunched forward. "Today we discuss the modern malaise of Mike Nichols' *The Graduate*," she imitated.

Olivia laughed loudly. "He used the word malaise to describe *everything*! I still don't really even know what it means," she confessed. A flurry of people entered the bar at once; the surrounding space was beginning to fill up fast.

Margot seemed to notice too as she sat up straighter and fluffed out her hair. "It's that stuff you put on a sandwich before you add the toppings," she declared.

Olivia burst out laughing again. It almost made her forget about Gwen. Almost.

"Margot, I have to tell you something," sighed Olivia. She didn't want to say it. She didn't want to start crying in the bar. She'd spent far too much time on her makeup to ruin it over something she couldn't change.

"What?" Margot inquired. "Are you thinking of going blonde again?" She patted Olivia's hair over the table. "Please don't, it didn't actually look that good. Wait. Are you," she immediately put a hand to her own stomach, "… pregnant?"

"What! *No!*" exclaimed Olivia. "No! I'll tell you!" She looked out at the sea of people. "I *need* to tell you." She felt her bottom lip begin to tremble. "Gwen's moving … to London."

Margot put a hand to her mouth. "Oh my god! When?"

Olivia tried to hold her expression very still. "The end of the month," she nearly whispered.

"Holy shit! That's so soon," exclaimed Margot. She frowned and looked Olivia in the eyes. "Liv, what are you gonna do?"

Before Olivia could answer, she turned to see Lucy walk through the door with Luke. Their friends Jasmine, Drew, and Evan trailed closely behind. Margot smiled and waved before lowering her voice. "Do you want to go somewhere else and talk about it? We can tell Lucy we'll be right back."

"No, no it's okay. I can't think about it." Olivia hesitated. "Let's just have fun, okay?"

They were hit with a wave of fruity perfume. "It's me! The birthday girl is here!" announced Lucy. She flung her arms around Margot and Olivia. "So glad you ladies made it! Let's go to my table!"

Margot grabbed Olivia's hand as the group walked deeper into the bar. "Let's hang this weekend, okay? We can talk about it then." She squeezed her hand. "I'm here for you."

What would she do without Margot? She smiled gratefully at her friend.

They followed Lucy in her sequined dress and a birthday sash and very high heels. There wasn't an occasion she didn't like to celebrate, especially when it was about her. Lucy had set up a private table near the back bar complete with balloons, champagne, streamers, a cake, and sparklers. *How much did this cost?*

Just Say Yes! was a surprisingly large bar in the West Village. It had two floors, the downstairs primarily for dancing, and three counters to order drinks. It gave off cocktail bar meets I-have-my-dad's-Amex-card vibes. Very popular for the high-rolling, post-college crowd. Olivia had come here after accepting her job offer for *Happy Hour* with Margot and Lucy and spent the night accepting drinks from men and dancing until they were sweaty and tired. They'd ended with pizza from the ninety-nine-cent shop around the corner and sat on the curb eating as the sun rose. It felt like that was much longer than just a year and a half ago.

The group took turns toasting Lucy, taking shots, and bribing the DJ to play Rihanna. Big, oafish Drew insisted on having a margarita in one hand and a slice of cake in the other: "Guyssss, sweet and salty!" No one told him he had icing on his nose. Just about every guy in a four-foot radius hit on Margot, and Evan ripped his pants attempting to "get low." Olivia was actually enjoying herself and this Scott-free evening. The friend group felt lighter without him.

While they were dancing, Lucy pulled Margot and Olivia to the side. "I have a s—secret," she slurred. "Luke and I are moving in together!" They hugged her excitedly. At least someone was having luck with a roommate. Olivia excused herself as a wave of sadness overcame her.

Whether it was from her sixty-hour work week or her three tequila sodas, at nearly two o'clock in the morning Olivia tripped coming out of the bathroom. She caught herself on the edge of a nearby table.

"Did you just fall for me?" a male voice asked over the pounding music. She rolled her eyes. That was such a Scott joke. She adjusted her dress and yanked up the tops of her boots. It kind of sounded like Scott, too. But it couldn't be. He had RSVP'd "No." Slowly, Olivia turned toward the voice and found herself face-to-face with the one person she didn't want to see.

His green shirt matched his twinkling eyes. The neon "bar" sign illuminated his smile.

"What are you doing here?" she inquired, doing her best to appear unfazed. Olivia was hardly a "cool" girl, but she could pretend.

"What happened to hello? How are you? Nice to see you?" Scott teased back.

"It's not nice to see you," she retorted.

"My business trip was canceled." He stirred his drink with his straw. "Come on, Olivia." His eyes traveled over her dress down to her boots and back up to her face again. "You look nice."

Olivia's cheeks felt hot. "Everyone's on the dance floor," she stated, smoothing her hair.

"Lead the way," he said as he gestured ahead.

They slowly walked toward the mass of dancing bodies. Olivia felt Scott put his hand on the small of her back, sending out waves of radiating tingles.

She looked around for Lucy or Margot but couldn't find them. She started swaying to the music instead, feeling Scott's hands move from back to her waist. Now was definitely the time to send herself home.

She turned around and faced Scott instead. They continued dancing, finishing the song, and then another, and another. Scott hadn't moved his hands from her hips. Maybe they *could* be friends? She felt Scott pull her closer, she wrapped her arms around his neck. But friends didn't dance like that. *Did they?*

"So you changed your mind?" Olivia wondered drunkenly into his ear.

"Huh?" Scott answered back, shouting over the music.

"You know." Olivia leaned closer, feeling more confident. "About being together."

She felt his body stiffen, his hands drop from her waist. "Olivia, we're friends. I figured we could still … you know."

Her arms fell from his neck as she took a step back. "What? No!" she commanded. Her anger was quickly replaced by embarrassment. *You are so stupid, Olivia*, said the voice in her head. She tried to remain in control. "Is that all I am to you?"

Scott stared back, answerless.

She abandoned him on the dance floor. Where was Margot? Lucy? Luke? She searched the back room but all she found were remnants of rainbow cake smeared on the floor and popped balloons.

"Where are my friends?" she cried into the abyss of gyrating twentysomethings.

"I'll be your friend," offered a bearded man in a beanie and red flannel.

"Ew, never, Paul Bunyan!" Olivia shrieked before pushing past the crowd and out the bar door, escaping into the cool air. She walked along the sidewalk as she felt tears begin to build.

Why did she think they could really just be friends? She closed one eye as she scanned the street for a taxi. She just wanted to go home. To forget about Scott and move on like Margot had said. Was it going to be like this every time she saw her friends?

She climbed into the backseat of an empty cab and didn't pick her head up out of her hands until the driver said, "Lady, this is you."

Tears wet the neck of her black dress as she twisted her key into her apartment door and let her purse fall in the hallway. She let out a sigh of relief when she opened Gwen's door and saw her sister curled in a tiny ball in her bed, the light from the hall illuminating her face. She was smiling in her sleep.

Olivia unzipped her boots and crawled into bed next to her. Gwen rolled over and draped a warm arm over Olivia's back.

"I'm sorry," Gwen whispered.

CHAPTER 5

The first boy Olivia ever liked was Connor Williams. As in like-liked, not just a little crush. He was tall, played soccer, had flowy dirty blond hair, and was one year older. A junior in high school while she was a sophomore. She thought it was very edgy of her to go for an older man. It made her feel mature. They were in AP biology class together, and it was there under the dim light of the Bunsen burner that Olivia fell in love.

Connor was smart, well-liked by his fellow classmates, and had a knack for making the people around him laugh. That's what Olivia loved most. He always seemed to be smiling. Olivia, who also deemed herself humorous, thought they would be the perfect pair. Always smiling, always making each other laugh.

The day Connor and Olivia were put at the same lab table was the same day Olivia made the varsity lacrosse team. Only two sophomores made the team that year, and Olivia was happy the second spot went to Carly, one of her closest friends. Carly's mom took the girls out to ice cream to celebrate that evening, gushing to everyone in the parlor that she was with Jefferson High's two youngest lacrosse superstars.

Connor's big blue eyes stared into Olivia's as she set down her books next to his in class.

"I heard you made varsity." He smiled effortlessly. "Congrats!"

Olivia looked down at her pencil case for a brief moment to hide her grin. "Thanks," she replied. "Somehow it was easier than getting Mr. Walsh to end class on time."

Connor laughed. She loved the sound of his laugh, deep and hearty. She loved even more that *she* made him laugh.

From there, the door to their blossoming relationship opened. *First we flirt in class, then we hang out by his car after school, and by May he'll be asking me to junior prom.* Olivia had planned their whole relationship in her head and was excited every time it seemed to stay the course. She and Connor got along even better than she'd imagined.

Talking in class proved to be difficult at times, but Olivia was surprised by how much fun they had mapping out Punnett squares, labeling the parts of the cell, and even dissecting their formaldehyde-soaked cat. It *was* AP biology after all.

Connor thought the dead cat was gross, with good reason, but Olivia was mesmerized. Of course she felt bad, but the cat was already dead! Plus, she'd never seen an actual kidney before! She found the entire dissection fascinating. There were so many layers, so many intricate pieces to notice and consider at once. Connor had, quite quickly, given her full control of the scalpel in exchange for taking notes for her all week. She liked that he knew she wasn't afraid of things, and that he'd offered to make even for his lack of participation.

At the end of the week, Connor was digging through his backpack when the bell to end class rang. "It looks like I forgot your notes," he speculated. His big blue eyes met hers. "They must be in my car. Come by after school and I'll give them to you." Olivia's heart did a flip. He was asking her to hang out by *his car*. Everyone knew couples hung out by their cars together before driving home. It was the one place teachers weren't hovering and parents weren't bothering between school and home.

Olivia played it cool when the final bell rang and made sure to finish a long conversation with Carly about that night's big game against Hamilton High, their rival, before heading to Connor's car. She knew it was the blue Camry, they'd talked about it before, debating whether people should name their cars or not. They both agreed that if he *were* to name his car, it would be "Charles," as in Charles Darwin, whose "survival of the fittest" theory applied quite well to Connor's worn down but sturdy Camry. But of course, that was just one of their many inside jokes.

Olivia saw Connor leaning against the side of Charles as she walked across the parking lot.

"For you, Meredith Grey," said Connor, making a sweeping gesture as he placed the notes in her hands. "Thanks for sparing me from cat guts."

She laughed and examined the notes. Connor had very neat, tiny handwriting. "I still think you missed out, but thanks for these."

She pretended to shuffle through the papers to cover the awkward silence that followed. *Now what?*

Connor adjusted his stance against the car and cleared his throat. "So, I'll be at your game tonight."

"You will?" blurted Olivia. The game already had enough pressure. She felt a mixture of dread and excitement as she looked at Connor.

"Yeah," he answered. "A few of the guys on the soccer team wanted to go since it's such a big game," he explained.

"You know, paint our chests, bang on trash cans. Manly stuff."

He shrugged. His hair fell into his eyes as he smiled again. Olivia nervously pulled on her ponytail. "Cool." She smiled. "Will you cheer if I score?"

"*When* you score," Connor corrected.

"Right." Olivia laughed. She saw Connor fiddling with his keys. "Well, thanks for these," she offered, waving the notes in the air. "See you tonight!"

Olivia scored two goals that night. Connor wouldn't shut up about the win the next day, describing each of her goals back to her. It was all the affirmation she needed that he liked her. Junior prom was just over a month away, and she now fell asleep at night thinking about all the ways he could ask her.

A couple weeks later, the soccer boys attended her last home game of the season. They came down to the field at half time, holding pieces of poster board. Olivia watched from her team's circle as five of the boys, clad in paint and Jefferson High School T-shirts, formed a straight line across center field. They each slowly lifted their poster above their head, to reveal the letters of the word "PROM?" written out in big, blue sharpie. Connor appeared at the end of the line holding a bouquet of flowers. The small crowd went wild. So did the butterflies in Olivia's stomach.

Olivia was glad her parents weren't at the game. Her mother would be asking a million questions that night at dinner about Connor. Of course, Olivia would allow her to finally meet him at prom. She could only imagine the ways he'd make her mother laugh. She grinned as Connor walked nearer and sat up straighter.

Olivia could see the sweat on his brow. He was nervous. He approached the circle in which the girls' team sat. Olivia tried to hide her smile. She wished Connor wasn't asking her when she was sweaty, but they'd laugh about it later. She wanted to pinch herself. She couldn't believe her plan had been followed. That reality, for once, had lived up to her imaginations.

Connor was mere feet away from her now. She saw the flowers were beautiful red roses. *Romantic!* Olivia tried to catch Carly's eye—only she knew how much Olivia liked Connor—but Carly's gaze was down on her cleats. Olivia focused back on Connor who had now arrived at the base of their circle. She felt her chest tighten. The mixture of dread and excitement. Any moment now. She readied her hands on the grass to help her stand up.

He cleared his throat. Ran a hand through his hair. The boys cheered.

"Michelle." He blushed. "Will you go to prom with me?"

Olivia pushed off the grass. *Wait. Michelle?* Her knees buckled as she fell back. She watched in slow motion as Michelle, the senior captain, giddily jumped to her feet and ran to Connor, throwing her arms around him. Olivia fought to keep her face expressionless as Connor handed Michelle the flowers and returned her hug.

Michelle held the bouquet close, a huge smile on her face. The fans clapped and the boys whooped and the girls awed. Carly looked at Olivia. Olivia cast her eyes away, mortified and embarrassed.

Olivia finished out the second half dropping nearly every pass, missing every shot, and getting called offsides again and again. She wasn't the type to turn misfortune into aggression. Instead, she wanted to curl up in her bed and cry.

"Olivia! What's going on?" her coach shouted from the sidelines. She was subbed out, on the bench until the final whistle blew. She didn't care.

Connor had come to her games because, just like Olivia, he too had a crush on someone older. She felt so stupid, so naïve to think he actually liked *her*. *He probably thinks I'm a little sophomore who likes to play with gross cat guts.* Olivia hated how she'd misread the signs: all their laughs, their conversations, their inside jokes. It had probably meant nothing to him.

The smile on Michelle's face remained etched into Olivia's memory as she fell asleep that night. The look of someone who felt worthy, accepted, wanted. Olivia vowed she'd never make a fool of herself again.

CHAPTER 6

Olivia awoke in dire need of water. She stood in front of the open refrigerator pant-less, aware the cold was spilling onto her bare legs, but she didn't feel it. She was in a daze. As if it was an out of body experience, she looked down at herself from atop her white kitchen cabinets. She saw below a small girl in a big gray T-shirt, white socks, slouched shoulders. *Is that really what my hair looks like from the back?* She'd lived this out-of-body feeling before. It was always after something very big. Like walking out of the SATs, or choosing her first city apartment, or finally getting to meet Violet Jones. They were moments that seemed so powerful that when they were done, she often felt as if the experience had been lived, but not by her.

A jar of pickles fell over on the shelf and snapped Olivia back into herself. She realized she'd been swinging the refrigerator door. The blueberries inside were moldy, cucumbers shriveled, eggs expired. Besides that, there were only condiments. Olivia and Gwen equally hated cooking. She sighed and filled a glass with cold water from the Brita and shut the door. Gwen was out—she could tell because all the lights were off.

Olivia grabbed the jar of peanut butter and crackers from the cabinet, tucked them under her arm and returned to her room, catching a glimpse of her reflection in the hallway mirror. Her eyes were swollen, red, puffy. Her dark brown hair was curled at the ends, yet greasy on top. Her skin was a dull, pale beige. Despite sleeping ten straight hours, she looked like she needed a nap. She felt like she needed one, too. Perhaps sleep would be easier than dealing with the creeping thoughts in her mind. She pushed her old water glasses aside to make room for her fresh glass on the nightstand and climbed back into bed.

Slowly slathering each cracker with peanut butter, Olivia watched the crumbs fall into her in bed. More piled up with each bite, gathering along the folds in her white sheets. *Gross*, Olivia thought and picked up another cracker. She reached for her phone.

"Breaking the news to Meredith today, be back tonight."

Gwen had texted. Olivia frowned.

Another message from Margot:

"Come over any time after four."

She turned her phone face down and lay back onto her pillow.

At half past four, she woke up. The apartment was dark. Gwen still wasn't home.

Olivia rose and scooped the crumbs from her sheets into her hand, gathered the empty glasses on her nightstand, and returned her snacks to the kitchen. She took a long, hot shower, then finally replied to Margot:

"On my way."

Margot lived in a studio in the Lower East Side, or "LES" as natives called it, which was loud, chaotic, and trendy in an expensive-grunge way. It was home to popular restaurants, cool bars, eclectic shops. There was always something going on in LES, and it usually started after midnight. The sidewalks were narrow, the buildings slenderer, the energy of the streets palpable; the neighborhood was pretty much how she'd describe Margot, an NYC native with uncapped energy and an edge. City kids *always* had an edge.

Margot's apartment building was a six-floor walkup, toeing the border to Chinatown, with steps so steep Olivia believed each one actually equaled two. The whole place was on par for a listing titled "prewar, cozy, with sink in bathroom!" It was sad how that wasn't always a given in New York City.

She knocked on her friend's door and was greeted by Margot within seconds. "Every time I climb these stairs I'm winded," gasped Olivia.

Margot laughed and ushered Olivia inside. They sat on her emerald green velvet couch.

Olivia noticed even more art had been added to Margot's wall behind them. With framed photographs and canvases of all different sizes, the wall acted as a rotating mood board for Margot's life. She loved bright colors, odd shapes, eye-catching patterns. The busier the better. Margot worked in PR, usually with small fashion brands and expensive handbag designers. Her apartment decor perfectly reflected the chicness and flurry of her lifestyle. Photos of old Vogue campaigns, magazine covers, abstract designs, a stolen "Girls Girls Girls" sign from a college spring break trip.

"How are you feeling?" Margot asked as she tugged on the zipper to her yellow sweater. She leaned back and put her feet up on her acrylic coffee table, her purple fluffy slippers matching the candleholders.

"Shitty," Olivia remarked, kicking her feet out of her shoes. She still had a lingering headache and her eyelids felt heavy.

Margot nodded. "Gwen leaving is really tough," she consoled.

Olivia sunk deeper into the couch and ran her hands through her hair. "Honestly, I'm really upset about Scott, too," she admitted. She told Margot about the rest of their night, nervously picking at her nails while she spoke. She hated how things had ended with Scott.

"But nothing happened?" clarified Margot. Olivia shook her head. "Then, so what? You guys aren't dating."

Olivia quickly turned away. "Jeez, Margot, I know." She resumed examining her nails.

"Sorry. Too harsh?" said Margot, patting Olivia's arm. "I forget that you're fragile when it comes to dating." Olivia forced a smile; she hated when Margot said that. It made her feel like she was doing everything wrong. "Do you want some water?" Margot asked. She stood up and walked into the kitchen.

Olivia nodded. "I'm not fragile. I'm just confused!" She sunk into the couch again. "Sure we weren't dating, but I don't understand why he suddenly can't be with me. Nothing happened!"

Margot presented her with a glass of water and sat back down on the couch. "I think guys like Scott can sense when things are getting serious," she said. "And he probably freaked out. Trust me, you're better off."

Olivia thought she and Scott could have at least talked about it more. Not only was their semirelationship ruined, but their friendship was too. She was hurt he didn't seem to mind at all.

"What am I supposed to do?" groaned Olivia. She stretched her legs out in front of her and noticed her white sock had a small hole near her pinky toe. "Avoid our friends? It's impossible to see Lucy and Luke without him there."

Margot finished a long sip of water. "You'll find someone else," she said. "He's not the boyfriend type."

Olivia was taken aback by Margot's diminutive comments. Where was the pep talk, the advice? Olivia had spent *hours* listening to Margot talk about *her* guys. Usually the ones she'd picked up at a work party, or met on a fire escape at a housewarming, or while petting the bodega cat waiting for a bacon, egg, and cheese bagel (if petting the bodega cat was how she was supposed to meet men these days, Olivia was definitely going to die alone). Was Margot downplaying this or was Olivia overreacting?

"That's an easy thing to say," Olivia said quietly. A few moments of silence passed as Margot scrolled through her phone. It hurt her that Margot had nothing more to add.

"Who are you texting?" Olivia finally asked. Between Margot's alpha energy and confidence speaking her mind, she had no problem getting men's attention. The issue was they couldn't keep hers. Margot remained under the spell of her phone's screen. Olivia decided to check her email. There was a note from Andrea with the subject line:

"Monday's To-Do List."

Olivia instantly felt her shoulders tighten, her stomach churn.

"Jared," Margot stated, finally resurfacing. "We've only gone on one date, but we've been chatting. I wasn't gonna say anything until it got more serious. Remember that psychic in the West Village told me not to date any guy whose name begins with the letter 'J,' so I'm taking it slow." Olivia realized the topic of Scott was over. Maybe she was making it into a bigger deal than it needed to be.

"What happened to Victor?" Olivia asked halfheartedly.

She missed the days in the city where she and Margot would use their weekends exploring. They'd go shopping in SoHo or thrifting in Brooklyn. Have coffee in the West Village or visit the Balto statue in Central Park. Now it seemed Margot's weekends were full of men from the internet. Even when Olivia had been seeing Scott, she'd always offered time for Margot.

"He went back to France." Margot picked up her water and took a sip. "But you know what? I could have *sworn* I saw him walking around last weekend near the fountain in Washington Square Park."

"Oh, man," offered Olivia. She felt her headache coming back and knew she wasn't in the mood for the saga of Margot's dating life.

"He had that ugly dog anyway," continued Margot, staring at her wall of art. She stood up and straightened the edge of a frame. "I'm just having fun," she declared, speaking more to herself than Olivia. "It's better when you don't take it so seriously, trust me."

Olivia stood and refilled her glass of water. She also helped herself to an Advil from the kitchen drawer. There was nothing that Olivia didn't take seriously. She cared enormously about everything she did. Besides, Scott was nothing like Jared or Victor who disappeared as quickly as they were found. He'd made it longer than any other guy she'd seen since moving to New York. Margot knew that. Olivia felt herself getting annoyed. Maybe it was almost time to return home.

"I'm not like that. I don't do anything half-baked," Olivia responded as she returned to the couch. She stuck her feet into her shoes.

"You should try it sometime," offered Margot, who was still assessing her wall art. She smiled at a newly added portrait of a Victorian woman sipping a piña colada.

Olivia would've never gotten her job at *Happy Hour* if she hadn't worked so hard to be noticed by Atlas. She didn't beat out hundreds of other candidates because her work ethic was "half-baked." Sometimes she feared she'd never have anything if she didn't give her whole self to everything she cared about. The same was true for dating, which she knew was what Margot was really talking about. But to Olivia, it was all the same. All things worth caring about required enormous effort.

"Well, not today. I do everything fully baked," Olivia responded firmly.

Margot eyed her suspiciously as she turned around, a smile on her face. "You do everything fully baked?" she questioned. "You're fully baked all the time?"

They both burst into laughter.

"Wanna watch *Drag Race*?" Margot asked. Olivia nodded, figuring she could stay just a little longer. She reached for a blanket.

~

Several hours later, Olivia returned to an illuminated apartment. She noticed Gwen curled up on the couch, a glass of tea on the side table to her right. A hardcover book was in her hands with the title: *Moving to London: A Yankee's Guide to Crossing the Pond.*

Olivia paused at the edge of the couch. "That's a very specific book," she remarked.

Gwen dog-eared the page and closed the cover. "Meredith had it waiting for me. She said she knew this day was coming," explained Gwen with a cautious smile. She sat up and patted the cushion, signaling for Olivia to join her.

"Well that makes one of us," Olivia said, sitting down.

"Still mad?" Gwen took a sip of tea and hugged her knees.

"I'm not mad," said Olivia slowly. "I'm sad." She looked at her poor picked-over nails. "About a lot of things."

Gwen stared at her with her big hazel eyes. "Me too." She touched Olivia's arm and set down her tea. "Look Liv, whatever happened with Scott. It's his loss. You'll find someone better."

Olivia felt exhausted. She was tired of hearing this. The simple truth was that one person she cared about very much and another person she *thought* she cared about very much were no longer going to be there for her. It sat heavy on her shoulders and ached down to her stomach.

"You have a habit for putting your energy into the wrong people," continued Gwen, sensing Scott was the greater source of Olivia's dismay. "You don't need to change, you just need to change the ones you pick." She smiled softly. "You're great just the way you are."

Olivia rolled her eyes. "Thanks, Mom."

CHAPTER 7

"Out of wine and out of time!" declared Violet Jones. "That's all we've got for today. Happy Friday! What a week it's been!"

Olivia silently agreed. It *had* been an eventful week; she was relieved the days had passed by quickly. Besides the news cycle being busy, Olivia had started searching internet groups for a new roommate. She'd arranged for several upcoming coffee meetings in hopes she could find one not-crazy girl.

She closed out of Friday's rundown and stared at Violet's perfect hair and bold smile on the Control Room screens, noticing Andrea next to her was doing the same. There was no denying Violet's screen presence.

"We've spoken with Senator Warren, heard new music from Taylor Swift, and even learned how to whip up eggless egg salad!" continued Violet. Olivia grimaced, imagining the smug look on Smith's face. After the widespread social media success of his breadless bread segment, Ken had asked him to think of more food substitutions. His latest (and grossest) recipe find had landed him a spot in the Friday Wrap-Ups. Only the most exciting, most-viewed segments were mentioned again during Violet's end of the week sign-off. Olivia had stayed late Tuesday and Wednesday helping Smith with research, photos, and B-roll. She was proud it did so well but noticed she didn't receive so much as a "thank you" from

Smith. He'd passed her by in the hall several times that week, refusing to make eye contact.

"I'm exhausted!" announced Violet as she laughed and mimed wiping sweat off her forehead. Olivia nodded in agreement. "See you all back here bright and early Monday morning," she promised. Her brown eyes found the center camera. "Until then, make every hour a *Happy Hour.*"

She flashed her Emmy award-winning smile and waved to the crowd. Her gold bangles dangled from her thin wrists, her teeth bright and white.

"Slide in the outro music," Pete announced into his headset. He began to move his hands as if he were leading an orchestra. "We're off the air in ten … nine," he counted from his seat in the front aisle of the control room.

Andrea sat to his left, spewing praise and compliments into Violet's earpiece.

"Add the sponsorship graphic," Pete directed. Olivia watched Violet's wave be replaced by an image. Her stomach immediately sank. Her eyes grew wide.

"What the hell is that!" Pete shouted and jumped to his feet.

"Take it down! Take it down!" shrieked Andrea, her chair bumping into Olivia's as she yelled.

"What is that?" questioned Ken from his seat in the middle row of computers. "Is that … an egg?"

Where there should've been a collage of their sponsors' logos was instead a photo of a large white egg with a red X through it. Olivia immediately recognized it as the image they'd used during the eggless egg salad segment.

Pete shook his hands furiously at the screens. "Go to black!" he commanded to the Technical Director seated to his right. The man quickly operated the large switchboard in front of him, sending the show into early commercial.

"I said the *sponsorship* graphic! Where did this come from?" thundered Pete as he threw off his headset.

"I'm calling the graphics department now," said Andrea, picking up the phone next to her.

Pete banged on the desk in front of him. "I'm sure the production assistant didn't check the rundown," he hissed and rubbed his temples. "Sloppy kids."

Olivia felt her stomach turn to knots. Was Pete referring to her? Why didn't he know her name? She checked the graphics, but she didn't *make* them. There was a whole graphics department for that. Between running scripts and printing Violet's notecards and finding last-minute props, she *always* checked the images in the rundown. Olivia had no idea how this could've happened. She was certain everything had looked correct that morning.

Andrea angrily slammed down the phone. "Graphics isn't answering. What else could they possibly be doing! Braiding each other's hair?" she scoffed. She turned toward Olivia, her sharp features accentuating her scowl. "Olivia, I need you to be always checking graphics. It is *extremely* important," she added condescendingly.

Olivia nodded and chewed on her cheek as she frantically clicked through the graphics folders again. Pete continued to grumble as she checked each and every segment, praying this wasn't her mistake. How could she get promoted to associate producer if she couldn't keep simple graphics in order?

"Andrea?" spoke Olivia nervously after she checked the final folder. No matter how it got on air, this mistake didn't come from her. "There isn't a photo of the egg from

Smith's segment anywhere in—" She was cut off by the ringing phone.

Andrea grabbed the receiver. "Yes, yes, fine." she nodded and rolled her eyes. "Okay then," she snapped into the phone. "Well, fix it for the later time zones."

She hung up aggressively again and spun her chair toward Pete. "The graphics team had it queued up by mistake," she explained. "It didn't come from our rundown." Pete nodded but still didn't look at Olivia.

Olivia unclenched her jaw.

"Olivia, I don't need your back talk by the way," sneered Andrea who quickly turned her attention to the middle row. "Ready, Ken? We have to prep for that ad sales meeting."

Nausea now filled her stomach. The little relief she had was gone. She felt even more embarrassed than before as she watched the remaining staff clear the Control Room. She'd only been trying to help.

Olivia waited until she was the last person left before she stood and gathered her notebook. While she walked toward the elevators she texted Hallie, deciding she needed a mood boost:

"Coffee?"

A woman in a gray suit waited beside her.

"Yes! Catering kitchen?"

Responded Hallie.

Olivia sent back a thumbs up as the elevator doors opened to reveal Ryan Reynolds. Olivia politely nodded as she stepped inside; the woman in the suit let out a small cry.

The doors closed and Olivia noticed the woman staring with lemur-like eyes at Ryan beside them. Her light brown hair had fallen into her face; she hadn't seemed to notice.

"Hi there," Ryan offered politely. The woman let out another little cry, practically beside herself with glee. Olivia had the fleeting thought that the woman may pee herself right there in the elevator.

The woman took out her phone. Olivia inched closer to the back wall, closing her eyes and praying the elevator would move faster. She heard the click of the camera and cringed.

The elevator came to a stop, and Ryan gave a curt nod as he stepped off. "Have a good one."

"You too, Ryan Reynolds!" she gushed back. "Oh my gosh!" she grabbed Olivia's arm with a claw-like grip as the doors closed. "That was *Ryan Reynolds!*"

"Yes." Olivia smiled.

"He's so cute!" She swiped through her cell phone as she bounced on her toes. "I need to text my husband!"

The doors opened and Olivia exited quickly, finding Hallie in the catering kitchen.

Today's small break before they began work on tomorrow's show was especially needed. They mixed their instant coffees, the two of them the only ones in the kitchen, as Olivia quietly recounted the incident in the Control Room.

"Pete's so lame," said Hallie in a hushed voice. "I hope he never meets my mom because she might try to marry him! He's the exact type of wet blanket she'd love." Hallie laughed at her joke.

Olivia chuckled out of politeness. She'd met Hallie's mom, Joy, a handful of times—once when Hallie had given Joy a studio tour and another when she had graciously taken the girls out for dinner. Olivia had only ever known Joy to be extremely kind, warm, and interested in her daughter's job. "So explain to me what a rundown is again, I think I've almost got it," she'd asked Olivia, who was shocked at the genuine enthusiasm displayed. "It's like a database of the whole show?" Olivia nodded in amazement. *Her* mom never asked about the rundown.

"I've been here for a year and a half! And he doesn't even know my name," whimpered Olivia as she opened the refrigerator door and pulled out the almond milk. The catering kitchen was hip to nondairy milks ever since J.Lo's team complained.

"I bet he doesn't know mine either," consoled Hallie, stirring her coffee. "And I've been here for three!"

"I'm sure he does," sighed Olivia. "Everyone knows you as Violet's right-hand woman."

"I guess," said Hallie as she took a sip from her paper cup.

Olivia put the milk back in the refrigerator. She leaned against the cabinets. "It's just after all this time, you'd think he'd know. It makes me feel worthless," she lamented. Pete and Scott seemed to have that effect in common.

Hallie nodded. "I get it. It's not like I want to be Violet Jones' assistant forever either."

Olivia wrapped a napkin around the paper cup to block the heat. "What do you want to be instead?" she asked as she raised the coffee to her lips.

Hallie chewed the corner of her cheek. "Well," she began. "I'm kind of hoping she makes me her producer one day."

"You should talk to her," suggested Olivia. "Set up a meeting. She seems more open minded than—"

They heard footsteps and turned toward the small kitchen door just as Andrea walked inside, her thin lips pursed and her hair still in its tight bun.

"Hi Andrea," said Hallie brightly. Olivia willed a smile.

They watched as Andrea pulled out a lemon yogurt and closed the door.

"Olivia," she turned, "can you run down and get a few dozen bagels before our ad sales presentation?"

She felt her cheeks flush for the second time that morning. Bagel runs were a staple of the interns' role.

"Actually, Andrea," chimed Hallie, as if she could read Olivia's mind. "I just got the interns' new cell numbers, want me to call one of them?" she asked. Hallie had a way of being assertive and incredibly sweet at the same time. *The interns have their own company cell phones now?* Olivia balked internally.

Andrea pulled open a drawer and rummaged through its contents. "That's very nice of you Hallie, but the interns are actually helping with the presentation. So, Olivia, I need it to be you." She pulled out a spoon and removed its plastic wrapping. "Get a bunch of different types of cream cheeses. You know, sun-dried tomato, vegetable, strawberry," she listed as she waved the spoon in the air. "Have fun with it."

Andrea then turned on her heel and walked out of the kitchen.

Olivia and Hallie stared at each other in silence until the clacks of Andrea's loafers disappeared.

"Actually, Liv," noted Hallie gently. "I'm gonna need you to be a doll and grab my dry cleaning for me." She waved her arms in the air. "You know, have fun with it!" She smirked.

Olivia laughed and threw out her coffee. "I better get going."

Twenty minutes later, Olivia delivered the bagels to the advertising sales presentation. She set them up quietly in the back of the wide conference room; the meeting looked like it was just about to start.

She unpacked the last cream cheese, cursing as the plastic top swiped across her blouse, leaving a mark of sun-dried tomato. She rubbed a napkin against it, but that only seemed to make the stain sink in deeper. With a huff, she took the last empty seat in the back row next to Wesley, the newly promoted producer.

"Just in time," Wesley whispered to her, smiling. She took in his wired-frame glasses, his smoothly combed back hair. He had on a bright yellow sweater over a white button-down shirt and immaculately shiny shoes.

He scooted his chair over to make more room for her. "This should be a fun one. Ad sales is trying to push us to promote more properties owned by Atlas," he said quietly.

Olivia looked to the front of the room, immediately recognizing the suited woman from the elevator as the leader of the meeting. Two blonde interns stood in her flanks, holding poster boards and grinning widely. An image of an upward trending line graph was on the projector behind them.

"What do you mean?" Olivia asked, adjusting her blouse to hide the stain.

He turned so he was facing her and whispered, "It means if we do a segment on new movies, we should only mention movies produced by Atlas." His light brown eyes narrowed and he shook his head in dismay. "Same for tech products, goods, anything owned by Atlas we have to start pushing more."

"Isn't that—"

"Disingenuous journalism?" he replied. "Yeah. It is." He rolled his eyes. Olivia liked that Wesley spoke so freely with her. It was a striking difference from how she was treated by Smith or Andrea. She figured Wesley couldn't be more than four or five years older than her.

"Alright, everyone! Bagels in the back, ad sales meeting in the front!" announced Ken, laughing at his joke. The staff obediently chuckled. "We'll start in five."

Olivia smiled at Wesley as he stood up from his chair and joined the crowd around the bagels. She scanned the room for Hallie. Suddenly, she felt a tap on her shoulder. A woman she had only ever seen in passing, who dressed in sensible shoes and long cardigans stood behind her. "Olivia?" she asked sweetly. "I'm Mary, with HR," she stuck out a hand.

Olivia had interacted with coordinators in HR before, but not Mary, who sat as the department head. Another wave of nausea rippled through her body. Had Pete really been that upset? Had Andrea overheard her and Hallie in the kitchen? Maybe Smith had said something since it was *his* egg segment?

"I love coming to these meetings," continued Mary, gesturing to the staff. "It helps me connect with the show and see some more faces! You in particular!" she winked. Olivia was thrown off by Mary's pep and energy.

"It's nice to meet you!" Olivia replied, trying to match Mary's gusto.

"Likewise! Olivia," she said as lowered her voice. "I noticed you applied for the open associate producer role. I'd like to invite you to an interview with Ken and Andrea next Monday." She grinned. "After the show, of course," Mary added with a laugh, although Olivia wouldn't be surprised if the interview *was* at three in the morning.

Mary's words took a moment to sink in. An interview for a promotion! The payoff she'd been hoping for, that made the bagels and the snippy comments worth it. She could actually be moving up the chain!

"Wow, thank you!" She felt a burst of energy shoot from her chest, down to her hands, her toes. She pressed her palms against her black pants. "Yes, that would be great!"

Olivia practically fell back into her seat. The incident with Pete and Andrea forgotten. The sun-dried tomato stain on her shirt out of memory.

CHAPTER 8

Olivia moved to New York City the way most people dream of: on a Megabus. With two oversized, overstuffed suitcases thrown into the underbelly of America's stickiest mode of public transportation, she left college to begin the next chapter of her life.

She'd accepted a job as an office coordinator at a small television production company, Proper Media, that mostly did corporate work and commercials. It wasn't fancy, it didn't pay well, but it was television. If she wanted to make it to Atlas, she knew she had to start somewhere.

The commute from her shared East Village apartment with Gwen to the quaint company offices in the West Village became one of her favorite walks in the city. She was instantly enamored by the hustle around her, the constant noise, the movement, the commotion. She took different streets every day just so she could see more.

There was something about New York. She couldn't stop looking at everything, listening to strangers on phone calls, smelling the fresh roasted nuts from the street carts. Every bodega, bank, bar, café, and newspaper stand called to Olivia's senses. She wanted to know what the locals were doing. Where they stopped to get coffee, what shoes they commuted in versus the ones peeking out of their bags. She'd grown up just an hour outside of Raleigh, North Carolina, and had frequently traveled to nearby cities like Charlotte and Charleston, but nothing was like New York. Nothing.

The first time Olivia pushed through the sturdy revolving doors of Atlas Broadcast Group, she was twenty-three and felt a chill run through her body. She'd received an email requesting her presence for an interview after applying diligently for months and promptly called out of work sick at Proper Media.

The lobby alone was impressive. The white marble floors. The grand chandelier. The impossibly high ceilings adorned with hand-painted frescoes of ancient Roman gods and blue skies. The gold leaf pillars along the edges of the walls. It resembled something out of a cathedral. Olivia could've been convinced Michelangelo himself had crossed the Atlantic and painted the masterpiece. She pulled her blazer tighter across her chest, unsure if it was the cold or if she felt the need for exceptional modesty in the hallowed grounds. The way her steps echoed on the marble, the sunlight spilling into the entryway, and the smile on the doorman's face all brought her a calm similar to how she felt in church on Christmas Eve with her parents and Gwen as a child, when everyone was exactly where they should be. As unbothered and undistracted as when they sang carols and dipped their bread in grape juice.

To Olivia, walking into Atlas *was* a religious experience.

She picked up her visitor badge from the security desk and walked up to the first elevator bank of many that lined the lobby.

"Um, excuse me," Olivia asked the guard. "Does this go to three?" He nodded and ushered her through the turnstile. She waited in front of the elevator. *Don't say um, Olivia!*

And speak slowly. Be confident! Gwen's advice from last night echoed in her head.

Gwen had spent all evening helping Olivia prepare for the interview. She sat on the couch as Olivia stood in front of her in the living room, repeating again and again her practiced responses of "her proudest achievement" and "a time when she had experienced adversity." Gwen had assured her these would all be standard interview questions for any industry. Although Olivia doubted how financial technology could be similar to entertainment.

"The trick, Liv," Gwen said folding her laundry on the couch, "is to answer these questions in the S.T.A.R. format. Situation, task, action, result. Be really clear, but be succinct."

"Right." Olivia nodded, pacing back and forth on the rug.

"But," Gwen sat up straighter, "that's what anybody would do. And you're not anybody. You have to stand out more. Show them why *they* need you." She folded a gray sweater and set it on her stack of shirts.

Olivia stopped pacing. "How do I do that?"

"Show them you know them," she replied. "Reference their history, their shows, their corporate values!" she exclaimed as she picked up another sweater. "I'm assuming you've researched all of this already?"

Olivia felt a wave of anxiety. "Gwen! Stop!" Olivia sank to her knees. "You're stressing me out!" She noticed a stray sock that had fallen onto the floor. She reached for it and squeezed it in her hand, hoping it'd absorb her anxiety.

"I already know those things! I know *everything* about their shows. They're all the ones we used to watch with Dad," Olivia explained.

"Even *Gator Guy?*" Gwen playfully retorted back.

"Especially *Gator Guy*," mused Olivia, tossing the sock at Gwen. "Gator done, one swamp at a time!" she quoted in a deep southern accent. Gwen let out a chuckle.

"I know everything there is to know about Atlas and *Happy Hour*," Olivia continued. "I want this job so badly I would give them my left arm!"

Gwen smiled. "Good. Now show them that."

Gwen's voice disappeared as the elevator doors opened to reveal the gold mirrors, plush walls, and carpeted floors with the Atlas logo. Olivia stepped inside, hoping her heels—well, Gwen's heels actually—hadn't picked up any stray dirt that would litter the carpet.

It had been a short ride to three. Barely enough time for Olivia to smooth her hair, wipe the corners of her mouth, and tell the jumping beans in her stomach to cool it. Her badge said "3E," and she wasn't entirely sure what that meant, but she decidedly set her face to a confident yet neutral expression and stepped out of the elevator. Surely there had to be directional signs somewhere.

"Looking for something?" chirped a small blonde in a houndstooth shirt and black turtleneck. She'd just walked out from the corner. Her eyes were blue and bold, her hair long and wavy. She seemed similar in age, but then again, everyone in television seemed to appear younger than they were.

"Hi, yes," Olivia stated firmly. "I'm looking for 3E."

"Oh!" gushed the blonde. "That's Ken's office. Here, I'll walk you." She gestured for Olivia to follow her.

"Thank you," Olivia replied as she followed the chipper girl down the hall. With each clack of her heel, she felt a beat of her pulse. She was seconds away from her interview. From getting a foot in the door. From a dream coming true. She forced herself to take a deep breath.

"Good luck!" the blonde smiled as they reached the end of the hall. "I'm Hallie by the way." She ushered Olivia to the door of the office. She winked before walking away.

Olivia took one last deep breath and knocked. She could see a figure rise from a seat through the clouded glass. The door opened to reveal a very tall, slender man with auburn hair. He wore a gray suit and had shiny black shoes. Olivia noticed the gold Rolex on his wrist as he stuck out a hand.

"Ken Whittington," he stated. "You must be Olivia."

"Yes. Nice to meet you, Ken," Olivia responded, echoing his name to show comprehension. Another note from Gwen.

She followed him inside the corner office where they talked about her education, previous work history, and favorite movies and TV shows. They even shared a laugh over their mutual obsession with youth cooking shows. "I was eating nothing but buttered noodles at that age! How do they do it!"

Ken included a few of the questions she'd rehearsed with Gwen, and even lobbed a trick question into the mix, which Olivia managed with ease.

"What do you think of competitor shows like *The Dr. Darren Show* or *Crime Time USA*?"

"Well, even though most people *think* that *Crime Time* is a competitor since it's on another network in the city, it's actually syndicated, as of course you know," she added with a smile. She saw Ken's eyes light up. "And its rights belong to Atlas, so it isn't a competitor at all! Actually, the show drives revenue further!" she finished with a flourish. Ken nodded approvingly.

It all seemed to be going well. Really well. She felt like she was in her element.

"Alright Olivia, I just have a couple more questions. Then I'll have to let you go as I have a meeting at noon," said Ken as he crossed his right ankle over his left knee. He sat back in his chair. "Why do you want to work in television?"

Olivia cleared her throat. Surprisingly, this was not a question she'd practiced with Gwen. She had a brief moment of panic, the anxiety in her chest swelled.

"I want to work in television because—" She paused to swallow.

"Because I love television!" she confessed. "I've always loved television. It's something almost everyone can relate to, no matter how young or old. It's a way we feel closer to one another. It's how I made friends in my college dorm—by bonding over the show posters on our walls. It's how I spent Wednesday nights with my dad growing up, laughing at *Gator Guy* after dinner."

She paused and looked around the office, grinning at all the different posters on the walls. They each depicted her favorite characters, settings, scenes, time periods. She had a memory tied to each one. "It was the only show we could ever agree on, actually. We have wildly different tastes, but I think if there's anyone who loves TV more than me it's him actually," she laughed. She saw Ken smile warmly in return.

"Television is how I spend my time alone when I feel sad and need a pick-me-up," she continued. "It's always there. I can always count on it. Everyone can. To create a shared bond with those around you, or to transport you far away when you need to turn your mind off." Olivia paused to tuck back a strand of hair that had fallen in front of her face. She realized she'd been speaking animatedly.

"I want to help create that. To be a part of making that feeling for everyone around me. That's why I want to work in television." Her voice was clear and strong, her mind grounded in the present. The words flowed freely and truthfully. There was no second-guessing herself.

"Thank you, Olivia. And lastly, why *Happy Hour*?"

"Oh that's easy," Olivia blurted. "I start every morning with *Happy Hour*! It's my time where I'm transported away from my to-do list, all the things on my plate, and I can just enjoy my coffee before diving into the day. I think the show is the perfect mixture of informative news, emotional interviews, and just plain … fun." She blushed at the end, kicking herself for her less than imaginative word choice. But Ken didn't seem to mind.

"Those are the exact words I would use to describe *Happy Hour* too, Olivia." He stood and reached a hand across the desk. "Welcome to the team."

The actors in the show posters rose to their feet and cheered. Gator Guy whooped, Trent from *Crime Time* clapped, *The Farm Family* whistled through their fingers, the pigs on their poster danced in circles. Even Violet Jones in the frame nearest the window gave a nod of approval. Pride and great relief surged through Olivia's body.

Upon stepping out into the crisp air, made cooler by the shade of the enormous Atlas tower, Olivia found her fingers dialing her dad's number. She heard the soft, low gruff of his voice.

"Olivia?"

"Hi Dad." She sat on a nearby metal bench. "I got the job." She felt her throat tighten. "I—I got the job at Atlas." A tear streamed down her face. She let it leave a trail down her cheek, dripping onto her blazer while she waited for his response.

"Honey," he replied softly. "I'm so proud of you."

More tears fell as Olivia scanned the building from top to bottom over and over again from her view on the bench. That was her building now. Her place of work. She belonged there.

Olivia realized the silence on the line was punctured by small sniffles. Was her dad crying too?

"My kid's gonna work at Atlas. Wow," he croaked.

"You'll have to come visit," she said. "You know, see the studios and everything once I'm in the swing of things."

"Gator done," he responded.

CHAPTER 9

Olivia's associate producer interview lasted ten minutes. It was interrupted by Smith needing approval on a segment from Andrea and left Olivia in a state of panic when Ken didn't offer her the job on the spot like last time. There were no trick questions. In fact, there were hardly any questions at all. Ken sat distracted behind his computer while Andrea explained the role to Olivia.

"You'll be in the edit room, of course, every morning, four o'clock. You'll be responsible for many of our interviews on tape, supporting B-roll, pulling last minute clips. Any research we need done ASAP will fall to you. Understood?" Olivia nodded. "You won't have anyone in the control room to catch your mistakes like you do now," Andrea snipped. Olivia's mind flooded back to the graphic incident. Were they still blaming that on her?

~

Weeks passed with no word from Ken or Mary. By mid-November, Olivia assumed the role had gone to someone else. While she wanted to ask her manager, she feared Andrea would frame it as "back talk" and strip her chances of promotion away completely.

On the Friday before Thanksgiving, Olivia slipped out of the office at five in the afternoon, set on avoiding another segment with Smith. It was her last night with Gwen. A sacred evening. She didn't want to get stuck on sausage-less sausage or waterless water or whatever else Smith could dream up.

A cluster of brown boxes were piled in the narrow hallway when Olivia arrived home. She shimmied between the stacks and peered into Gwen's room, spotting her sister on a stepstool in front of an empty closet. Gwen's hair was piled high in a messy bun that flopped from side to side as she ran her hand along the barren top shelf.

Olivia knew life would differ with a new roommate, but she just couldn't picture it. Gwen was everywhere in their apartment. Her books filled their shelves, her hair was in the sink, her Prada purse in Olivia's room. She had to remember to return that.

When Olivia and Gwen had moved in together in the East Village, they both experienced the joy of a doubled wardrobe and the comforts of their dynamic language they formed in childhood: an understanding through a look, an exchange with a gesture, the ability to finish each other's sentences and guess each other's thoughts. Their bond withstood their two-year age gap, ephemeral fights, stolen sweaters, and broken hair clips.

"Looks like you got just about everything," remarked Olivia.

The apartment already felt different. Emptier. Less warm. Hollow. The stacked boxes covered their framed prints of Italy and Spain. The soft gray rug in Gwen's room was tied up in the corner. Gwen's expansive closet to which Olivia generously helped herself had only hangers on the rack. Gwen's candles, books, framed awards from work were all boxed away. All traces of her were gone. Olivia tried very hard not to commit this sight to memory.

Gwen slowly stepped down onto their parquet floors and rolled down the sleeves of her sweatshirt. "I ordered us sushi," she said. "To have one last time before I go. Can you get it when they buzz? I just want to wash this dust off."

She padded into the bathroom and closed the door. Olivia heard the shower turn on. She hadn't moved from her spot in the doorway. If she walked farther into the apartment, if she kept moving, that meant time was really passing. That she was inching closer and closer to a life without Gwen. She didn't want that to happen. Maybe if she stood really still, time wouldn't tick by and Gwen wouldn't leave. The door buzzed.

Olivia regretfully turned to collect their sushi and brought it into their kitchen. She removed the tins from the paper bag and brought the chopsticks and miso soup containers to the living room, setting up their spread on the coffee table.

"Any word on your interview?" Gwen asked fifteen minutes later, sitting next to Olivia on the couch with chopsticks in hand. Her hair was wet and smelled like her expensive shampoo. Olivia realized she'd have to start buying her own soaps.

Olivia shook her head. "Not yet." She picked up a piece of spicy tuna roll.

Gwen chewed thoughtfully. "Do you think it's fair that they're making you wait?" She shook her head. "We don't treat our candidates like that."

Olivia reached for another roll. "I mean, I'll wait as long as I have to," she confessed.

Olivia sensed a theme in her life of wanting things that didn't eagerly want her back. Not that she'd *ever* compare

Scott to the likes of Atlas. *Happy Hour* was a dream she'd chased and made come true. She prayed this promotion wouldn't pass her by.

She sipped her miso soup. "Remember when we used to watch TV with Dad at night? And then go off and write our own plays and make our Beanie Babies act in them?" asked Olivia.

Gwen laughed. "How could I ever forget?" She smiled. "*Weekend at Beanies* was a box-office hit."

"I think that was our best one," giggled Olivia. She placed her soup on the coffee table and sat back farther on the couch.

She thought back to the dances and high kicks they'd make the little bears perform. Gwen's bedroom, always the main stage, would be covered in the plush toys by the end of the night. They'd beg their parents to watch their shows that sometimes stretched on and on. Despite their creative differences, the sisters always came together on the last act. Somehow every story ended with Gwen's Beanie Babies as the heroes. She had a way of planting ideas in Olivia's head and making her think they were her own.

Olivia reached for the blanket as she thought about Gwen's comment earlier. Her eyebrows furrowed. "What did you mean by 'fair'?"

Gwen looked up. She knew better than to play dumb. "That they treat you like that," she stated.

Olivia's face crumpled.

"Oh Olivia, chill! I was just asking. I don't know what's right for you!" argued Gwen.

"Of course you do! You always do," Olivia groaned. There Gwen was putting ideas in her mind again. "Like when you told me to pick lacrosse over soccer, or biology over chemistry."

Gwen closed her sushi tin. "Those are just things from high school!"

"Yeah, but I ended up being really good at them!" exclaimed Olivia. She stared at the empty take out containers on the coffee table. "You're always right and I hate it." She felt a lump forming in her throat.

"Stop, you're just getting mad to make this goodbye easier. Honestly, it's a fair tactic." Gwen smiled.

Olivia gulped as tears sprung to her eyes. "N—no one knows me better than you d—do!" she cried, burying her face in the blanket.

She felt Gwen reach over and pat her arm. It wasn't fair. Life in New York with Gwen was good. *Why does it have to change?*

Gwen handed her a takeout napkin.

"Look, it won't be that different," assured Gwen. "Except I won't be around to curl your hair anymore."

Olivia sniffed. "But I'll be alone here." She pressed the rough napkin against her cheeks.

"You won't be alone," said Gwen reassuringly. "And even so, you can be alone and not feel lonely." She took a deep breath and pulled a corner of the blanket over to her. "It has nothing to do with you, really," she stressed. "But I feel lonely all the time here."

Olivia placed the damp napkin down. "You do?"

"I mean, yeah," answered Gwen. "You love New York in a way that I just don't anymore." She picked at the hairs on the wool blanket as she spoke. "And the second I stopped liking it here, I started to feel like the biggest outsider," she confessed.

"I didn't know that," said Olivia quietly. She thought Gwen *liked* hearing about her crazy nights out with her friends, her celebrity sightings at work. She didn't realize it made her feel distant.

Gwen nodded her head. "That's partly why I took the role in London—to give myself the chance for a fresh start." She looked into Olivia's eyes. "I need to give it a shot," she stated.

Olivia studied her sister's face. It was the face she'd seen nearly every day for the last two years. It looked strikingly similar to her own. Olive skin, dark eyebrows. The only facial feature that varied was their eyes. Olivia's were a brown so dark they almost matched her pupils, while Gwen's were a softer, golden hazel. They were the same shade as their mother's, brown in the center and with a ring of gold along the edges. Olivia noticed a twinge of sadness in them. How long had Gwen been unhappy? Olivia was so busy thinking about Scott and work and how Gwen leaving would affect her that she never thought about why Gwen wanted to leave in the first place. Could she really be mad at her sister for wanting more?

Olivia squeezed Gwen's hand. "I know. I'll just miss you a lot."

Gwen moved closer on the couch and pulled Olivia into a hug. It made her feel safe, protected, like everything would be okay. When they parted she noticed tears in Gwen's eyes.

"Call me when you get there?" asked Olivia. "And then every day after that?"

Gwen laughed. "Of course I will. We'll talk every day. Promise."

CHAPTER 10

The ancient Roman gods stared down from above as Olivia repeatedly pressed the elevator button for the third floor. It had been one week without Gwen. Four weeks since her interview. And over a month without Scott. But who was counting?

She gave a great sigh and hurried herself inside when the doors finally opened. There was no sunlight, definitely no sense of calm, and no smile from the security guard—there was practically no one around at all. It was 5:55 a.m. after all. Meaning Olivia was ten minutes later than her normal extra-early arrival. She rushed to her desk and threw off her coat.

"I need graphics pulled for the new Guillermo del Toro movie."

Olivia jumped at the voice behind her. She turned to find Smith standing near, his gray shirt already showing signs of sweat.

"Sure, just a second," she gestured to the computer starting up.

He pursed his lips. "I also need you to confirm the updated intro script is in the rundown, check the pronunciation of the main character's name, find a prop bathtub, and tell me how to say water in sign language. As *quickly* as you can," he growled. He ran a hand through the imaginary hair on his head.

"I'll get on that, Smith," she responded. The computer screen was still black. She scrawled down his list of to-dos. *A bathtub?* "I just need a minute."

"You need a minute? *The Shape of Water* is going to win best picture of the year, this interview must be *perfect!*" he thundered. Olivia felt a spray of spit land on her cheek.

She quickly wiped at her face. "This was just a tough morning. I'll get to work as soon as I can," she explained, looking into Smith's beady eyes.

Olivia missed the days when she passed Smith in silence. Since she'd begun helping him with segments, Smith was treating her like his personal assistant. Especially in the mornings, which were already a busy time with her normal production assistant roles.

Smith laughed, "Let me guess, the party was too good last night to leave?"

Olivia gaped at him.

"You're a kid," he continued. "What else could you have going on?"

Smith turned and stormed off in a huff. Olivia watched him back away from his kill. The hunt over. The lion successful. She sat in shock, blinking back tears until her computer finally loaded.

The truth was she wasn't sleeping well. When her alarm clock had gone off that morning, she was in a groggy state somewhere between awake and dreaming. She just couldn't will herself to get ready. Olivia thought she'd enjoy the alone time before Gwen's space was filled by a stranger. But she was wrong. The tiny apartment somehow seemed too big without Gwen. Noises became unfamiliar—the creak of the neighbors walking overhead, the music that they played somehow growing louder and later, the buzz of the refrigerator. They startled Olivia and kept her on edge.

Despite going to bed even earlier than usual and adding an extra cup of coffee to her mornings, she couldn't quite shake the feeling of exhaustion that had settled in. She had mentioned her sluggish disposition to Margot, who had simply stated, "This whole city is tired. That's why everyone does drugs!"

Margot had agreed to sleep over for a few nights during the week so Olivia wouldn't be alone until her new roommate, Jess, arrived.

"This reminds me of finals week," Margot said one night, adjusting her pillow on the couch. Her long legs hung over its edge, her bright pink PJs peeking out from underneath the blankets. "When you and I were the only ones with a Friday final, and the whole dorm had cleared out, so we dragged your mattress into my room." She laughed. Olivia smiled and began to chuckle as she remembered the twin XL mattress getting caught in the door. They had collapsed in a fit of giggles, neither of them able to unwedge the bed as their laughs weakened their grips.

"Gwen wasn't kidding when she said she hardly saw you during the week," continued Margot. From the time Margot's work finished and she'd made her way from the PR firm in Columbus Circle to Olivia's, they only had about an hour of overlap before Olivia went to bed. Olivia tried to be quiet when she left for work in the mornings, careful not to wake Margot since she was doing her such a favor, but it didn't leave much time to talk or catch up. "How in the world do you go on dates during the week?" she called from the couch.

"I don't," responded Olivia as she wiped off her makeup with a cloth in the bathroom. She could see Margot from the reflection in the mirror. "You knew that."

"I guess," pondered Margot. "I just didn't want to believe it. I have a date tomorrow with a real estate broker by the way. I met him at a gallery opening last week."

Olivia wasn't sure if it was her lack of romantic prospects that made her feel this way, but lately all she ever felt from Margot was pressure and judgment about dating. Margot was still her best friend, her person, still kindhearted and silly and helpful. She was sleeping on Olivia's couch when she had a perfectly good bed at home for God's sake! Yet Olivia couldn't shake the inkling that Margot was becoming more and more obsessed with men. She was boy crazy!

Margot rearranged the blanket over her body. "Wait, when was the last time you had—"

"Margot, please!" interjected Olivia. She turned on the sink. "Don't remind me that I have literally no love life right now. It's humiliating."

It felt like another to-do list item: replace Scott. It sat heavy on her shoulders and reminded her that with Gwen gone, she was more alone than ever.

After her incident with Smith that Friday morning, Olivia was relieved when the show was over. Andrea hadn't mentioned any producers needing segment help that day, and Olivia hoped it would stay that way. She and Hallie had agreed to treat themselves to coffee in the Atlas cafeteria after the show. She felt her phone vibrate as she walked through the long halls.

"Gwen!" she answered excitedly, their daily phone call becoming a highlight of her routine. "Did you find a place to live?"

"Not yet," responded Gwen cheerfully, who was staying at a hotel until she found somewhere more permanent. "I'm viewing a few flats tomorrow afternoon actually." *Flats.* Olivia laughed internally.

"And your new colleagues are okay?" Olivia asked as she entered the cafeteria and headed straight to the coffee bar.

"They're great!" exclaimed Gwen. "Tonight they're taking me to a pub to celebrate my first week." *Pub.* Olivia could hear Gwen's smile through the phone. There was an energy to Gwen's voice that hadn't been there before.

"That's awesome. I'm really glad," Olivia answered. She surveyed the coffee selection in the cafeteria and adjusted the top of her corduroy skirt. One week without Gwen's closet and she'd already gone through all her best outfits. She wondered if Jess would be the type of roommate to share clothes.

"I don't have much time to chat today, I just wanted to check in," Gwen explained. Olivia could hear people speaking in the background and an eruption of laughter. Even Gwen's office sounded livelier.

"No problem," responded Olivia. She picked a dark roast and poured it into an Atlas-branded paper cup, taking care to only fill it halfway so the cashier wouldn't charge her full price. "Maybe we can talk again tonight?" She fumbled with the plastic lid.

"I have that pub thing, remember?"

"Oh, right, right," said Olivia quickly. "Okay, tomorrow then," she decided. She wanted to tell Gwen about Smith and get her opinion on his comments. Should she mention this to Andrea? Or Mary at HR? Gwen was always good with advice like that.

"Miss you," said Gwen softly.

"Miss you, too," answered Olivia. She put her phone back in her pocket, grabbed her hot coffee, and looked out across the high-top tables for signs of Hallie. She spotted her near the windows that overlooked Fifth Avenue when she collided into the back of a clipboard.

"Woah!"

"Oh, I'm so sorry!"

The clipboard dropped to reveal Wesley's face. "Olivia! Did I make you spill?" He wore a pair of thick-rimmed black glasses today.

Olivia assessed her white shirt, her corduroy skirt. "No actually! We're safe, all good."

"Thank god," breathed Wesley. "Here, let me get you a napkin anyway." He followed Olivia to the table where Hallie sat and handed her a stack of Atlas-branded napkins.

"Thanks," Olivia replied, smiling. In contrast to Smith, Wesley was by far the nicest of the producers. Probably because he was the youngest, the most familiar with what it felt like to pay dues.

"Hey Hallie," greeted Wesley, placing his clipboard on the table. "Thanks for saving me this morning." He turned to Olivia and explained, "Hallie switched out a page in Violet's research packet for me." He grinned. "A covert operation!"

Hallie laughed. "Indeed! No problem." She slid her coffee over to make space. "Want to join us?"

"Sure, if that's cool?" Wesley asked, reaching for another high-top chair. Both girls nodded eagerly. "I'm not used to this postshow grace period," he admitted. "When I was an associate producer I had no free time at all. My boyfriend said I was like a zombie. "

Olivia took a sip of her coffee and felt slightly queasy at the thought of her role getting even *busier.*

"Oh god, really?" she asked. "I interviewed to be an AP like a month ago. Still waiting to hear back."

"You'll be okay," assured Wesley. "I made it through!" He looked out the Fifth Ave windows and grimaced. "Besides, Grace—the night shift AP—has it the worst in my opinion. She works until like two in the morning. Her schedule is totally backward."

Olivia hoped she'd never get put on that shift.

They spent the next fifteen minutes talking about her interview, mornings in the Control Room, and overall life at Atlas, interjecting with little anecdotes about Andrea or Ken. Hallie nearly spit out her coffee when Wesley told them of the time Andrea complained his segment music was too "happy."

"Sadly, I have to run," Wesley added as he finished his story. "This was really fun. Same time next week?" he said with a wink.

They watched Wesley walk out the cafeteria doors and into the winding halls of Atlas. Olivia turned to Hallie. "Wesley is ... cool?"

"I was thinking the same thing!" she exclaimed.

"I wish I'd known him earlier," Olivia said, wiping her lips with an Atlas napkin. She noticed it read, "Happy 90th birthday, Atlas!" She looked up at Hallie. "That reminds me, what are you doing for your birthday this weekend?"

Hallie rubbed her lips with a tub of tinted lip gloss that she'd pulled from her pocket. "Well I'd normally go to Maryland and spend it with my mom," started Hallie. "We bake cookies, watch movies—*White Christmas* is our favorite." She smiled. "But, she is with her new *boyfriend* in Florida this year, so ..." Hallie's voice trailed off.

"We should do something! Let's go to brunch!" Olivia quickly interjected. "Maybe Saturday?" Hallie grinned. With that, they grabbed their empty coffee cups off the table and walked back to the office.

Whether it was mutual, or Olivia had willed it into existence, she'd managed to avoid Smith for the rest of the day. She was instead paired with Hank, an older producer her dad's age with deep-set eyes and rounded shoulders. They worked together on an upcoming segment on air travel hacks. She noticed he moved a bit slower, spoke quietly, and took his time selecting graphics and B-roll.

At four o'clock he tapped on her desk and said, "This intro is great, did you write this?" Olivia nodded, pride filling her chest. "Heck of an opening hook. You're a talented storyteller." She felt herself blush.

"Say," he continued, "haven't you been here since five?" She nodded again. "Well, skedaddle! I can finish up without you. You work such long days." Olivia almost cried.

"Thanks Hank, I appreciate it." She beamed. "Have a great weekend," she said, fighting the sudden urge to give him a hug.

Olivia packed her bag and began her walk home. Careful to avoid a green wad of sidewalk gum, she hopped over the curb and continued toward Third Avenue. She passed a couple intensely making out against a scaffolding beam. *Ew.* She passed another couple holding hands as they waited on the corner. *Also ew. People in love are gross.* She had just walked by Stinky's, an aptly named dive bar enjoyed by her friends, when she felt the familiar buzz of her phone through her coat pocket. She didn't recognize the number apart from the 212 New York area code. She paused in the doorway of a nail salon to answer.

"Olivia! This is Mary from HR. Is now a good time?" the caller said brightly.

Olivia's heartbeat quickened. She took in her surroundings: a taxi honking at a red light, a woman pushing a stroller, a kebab cart giving off a suspicious amount of smoke. "Oh! Yeah—yes," she stammered. "I'm just walking home so there may be some background noise."

"Getting an early start to the weekend I see!" chortled Mary. The smoke around the kebab cart seemed to double. It was growing by the second.

"Well, Olivia," she continued. "I'm calling because you interviewed for the associate producer role." Olivia felt her heartbeat quicken again. "Are you sitting down?" hummed Mary. Her singsongy voice told Olivia that she loved doing phone calls like this.

"Oh I can't hold it in any longer," gushed Mary. "Olivia, you got the job!" she announced ecstatically. The smoke rose higher and higher. It looked like the whole kebab cart was about to go up in flames. The owner of the stand ran out and started fanning the scene with a hand towel.

Olivia realized Mary was waiting for her response. "Oh!" she exclaimed. "Wow, thank you! That's great!" She was transfixed on the battle between the cart and the man as he fought back the fumes. "That's really exciting. I'm really excited. Thank you," Olivia repeated.

"You are quite welcome, Olivia!" answered Mary. "Before I let you go celebrate, Andrea has asked you to come in this Sunday to begin training. Four in the morning, that's when the AP starts," she explained. "Sound good?" It looked like the smoke was finally dying down. Its great clouds dissipated into the sky, puffs becoming smaller and smaller. Olivia watched the owner wipe the sweat from his forehead with the towel.

Olivia stepped out from the doorway and paused to look uptown, away from kebab commotion, the phone still pressed to her ear. There, in that moment, the Chrysler building tumbled to the ground, glass smashing everywhere, covering the streets in rubble. She blinked repeatedly until the destruction cleared.

"I can't wait," responded Olivia.

CHAPTER 11

Two weeks later, she was in the full swing of associate producer training, spending half of her day completing production assistant duties and the other half in seminars learning how to call the White House.

A text exactly one hour ago from Margot had coerced her into a "fun night out," which sounded like an oxymoron to Olivia, who just wanted to sleep. The longer days were exhausting.

"Please, please."

Margot wrote.

"It can be just us. A girls' Friday night out! Like old times!"

Olivia reluctantly agreed and Margot arrived shortly thereafter with a garment bag, a full tote of makeup, and a bottle of red wine. They donned fluffy robes, streamed girl pop bands from the Bluetooth speaker, and fell back into the routine of their early NYC days.

"One of our clients let me name a handbag today!" Margot announced as she applied blush in front of Olivia's gold floor length mirror.

"What did you name it?" A piece of Olivia's hair was wound around the curling iron as she sat at Margot's feet.

"The Margot, duh!"

Olivia laughed. "Of course." She released her hair from the curler and picked up another chunk, wrapping it away from her face.

Margot traded her blush for an eyeshadow palette. "How's training for your promotion going? And can I do your eyes?"

"Yes, but not too dark!" she answered, looking at the browns and reds in the palette skeptically. "Training is going okay," she continued. "It's … a lot." Olivia winced, thinking back to the phone call where she told her mom about her new role.

"Are you done reporting to that awful manager now?" her mom had asked hopefully.

Olivia had reassured her Andrea was still very much her manager. She'd also explained that her hours had shifted even earlier, and her hourly pay had only increased by one dollar, to fourteen an hour.

"Isn't Atlas a massive corporation? Why can't they pay you a living wage?" her mom prodded.

"It's just how it is," Olivia responded.

"Well, did you ask?" her mom pushed back. "I'm sorry, Olivia, but this promotion," she gave a long sigh, "frankly, it hardly seems like a promotion at all."

"Yes Mom, I did ask," snipped Olivia. "Why are *you* asking so many questions?" she rounded. "Why don't you just stay out of it, or I don't know, say congratulations like a *normal* parent!"

Olivia had angrily hung up on her. The excitement she'd felt when she first joined Atlas, the hope and promise she'd been so eager to share in the beginning, was now deflated. She knew her mom was comparing her to Gwen. The same Gwen who had been forgetting to call every day like she'd promised.

Her mom had called back. Olivia had pressed ignore.

"I thought you said you were ready to get over Scott," declared Margot, snapping Olivia back to reality. She took a sip of wine out of a *Happy Hour* mug. "This is step one," she stated, dipping her brush into the colors.

Olivia nodded slowly and checked her phone: still no message back from Gwen. She obediently closed her eyes. It was late in London now anyway. She wouldn't hear from her until tomorrow.

Margot began her methodical brushing and blending of eye shadow. It reminded Olivia of all the times Gwen had done her hair. It felt nice to be pampered. To have someone looking out for her, helping her, showing affection. Olivia tried to think of the last time she'd been hugged. Margot wasn't a big hugger, and neither was Olivia, but Gwen would hug all the time despite her protests. "People need to be hugged. It reminds us we are loved," Gwen used to say. The light strokes from the bristles on her face felt nice. Comforting.

There was a quiet knock on the bedroom door. "Come in!" called Olivia.

A small beanie-clad Jess poked her head inside.

When Olivia had first met Jess for coffee and heard she was a mechanical engineer from Minnesota, with a love of books and an affinity for candlemaking, she decided Jess was the one. Olivia would've bet all $232 in her savings account that Jess would *not* be the type to throw wild parties or bring home strange men. Plus she had a kind smile and seemed like a sweet girl.

Jess tentatively took a step inside Olivia's room, her curly hair peeking out from under her hat. "I'm going out. Have a good night!" She smiled. "Thanks for that book by the way, Olivia. Can't wait to read it."

"I hope you like it!" answered Olivia, who had noticed a copy of *Hit Refresh* by Satya Nadella, Microsoft CEO, on the staff bookshelf and had thought it'd be a nice gift for Jess. *Engineers like computers, right?* "Where are you headed?"

Jess took another step into the room. "I'm going with some coworkers to the Empire State Building. It's supposed to be really pretty at night." She smiled again.

Margot paused her blending of eyeshadows. "I've actually never gone to the top before," she admitted. Margot tapped Olivia's knee. "Have you?"

"No, neither have I," said Olivia as she opened her eyes and peered into the mirror.

"It's never even crossed my mind, to be honest," said Margot thoughtfully, wiggling the brush in her hand. "Jess, let me know how it is. Maybe I'll take my grandparents next weekend."

"Okay!" agreed Jess. She adjusted her beanie. "Well, goodnight," she said, carefully closing the door.

~

Forty-five minutes later, after two *Happy Hour* mugs of wine each and one small dance break, Olivia and Margot stood shoulder-to-shoulder in the mirror. Olivia had to admit, Margot made her brown eyes look deep and mysterious, popping against her olive skin with dark red and sienna colors.

"You look hot!" exclaimed Margot.

"I look average," she stated as she studied herself in the mirror. "Maybe slightly above." She smirked. Olivia wore black leather pants, black lace-up booties, and a chocolate brown satin halter. Margot was in all silver, down to her heeled boots. Only she could do aluminum-foil-meets-alien-vibes and still look cool. They grabbed their coats, hailed a taxi, and headed downtown to Flower Child, a recently opened bar in SoHo.

They entered through the vault-like door adorned with holiday lights and walked past the crowded plush couches and pink armchairs. Olivia was overcome by the sudden wave of heat. There was a U-shaped bar in the middle of the narrow establishment with clusters of hanging lights overhead. Half of the bulbs were a pink neon, giving a rose tint to the entire room. The bass was so deep Olivia felt the reverberation in the center of her chest. She grabbed a menu off the bar, staring at the tiny font. She squinted her eyes. *Am I aging already?*

"Two tequila sodas please with a twist of lime," shouted Margot to the bartender. "I like your beard," she added. He winked at her. Margot tapped Olivia on the shoulder and gestured to the ceilings. "Look up there!" There were rows of vintage flower vases that had been outfitted into disco balls.

"How cool!" Olivia nodded back enthusiastically. Probably too enthusiastically. A small pit had formed in the center of her stomach. She wanted to show Margot that she was still fun, that she was still worthy of a girls' night, but she felt overwhelmed. The lights, the music, the crowd: it was all too much.

"Let's go find you some cute guys!" Margot called in Olivia's direction. This was Margot's favorite game. Her face lit up as the disco balls swirled, catching the sparkle in her eye. They grabbed their drinks and drifted into the center of the bar. Margot in her silver ensemble stood tall, acting as a beacon of light for the men around them. Like moths, they began to circulate and hover.

Olivia felt a tap on her shoulder. "Hey," greeted a pale man with freckles. "Have we met before?"

She studied his eyes and his blonde hair thoughtfully. "I don't think so?" she answered. How much did she used to drink?

He laughed, "No, we haven't, but I just needed a way to introduce myself." He smiled wryly. "So, how's it going? I'm Nate." He took a sip of his beer.

"Nate! That's my mom's name," she exclaimed. He stared at her.

"I'm kidding." Olivia chuckled to herself. She and Margot used to think that joke was funny. "I'm good!" she continued. "Well, not really, I mean, it's so loud in here. And I could hardly read the menu!"

"Good point!" Nate shouted. "I guess we're due for an eye exam!" he joked.

Olivia laughed and took a sip of her drink. "It's like, I'm only twenty-five. I can't get old yet! I haven't even paid off my student loans!" she exclaimed. Nate nodded in agreement. "Or bought an apartment or met the love of my life. Like, let's hope I get married before I need reading glasses!" Olivia continued. Nate cocked his head to the side.

"I still have the rest of my life ahead of me!" She threw her hands into the air, sloshing her drink down her arm. "Oops." She laughed nervously. "And don't get me wrong, I *like* my job, but is that my career forever now? What about those people that quit corporate America and become yoga instructors? Will that be me?" Nate slowly backed away from Olivia until she was left standing alone. *What's his problem?* she thought, ignoring the notion that she'd overdone it a smidge. Where had Margot gone?

Olivia noticed the drink in her hand was empty and decided to re-up at the bar. As soon as she placed her elbows on the counter, a guy in a fleece vest tapped her on the shoulder. "Hey, let me get that for you," he offered.

He had vivid blue eyes. Even in the rose-colored bar lighting, Olivia could tell they were striking.

"Oh that's so nice. Thank you." She stuck out her hand. "Olivia."

"Matt," he stated. "I work at Morgan Stanley."

Olivia had a thing about guys that tied their job to their name. She'd dated this type of guy before, when she'd first moved to the city. The kind of guy whose dad or grandfather hooked him up with a job right out of college. Whose family owns a golden retriever somewhere in the suburbs of Pennsylvania. The kind of guy who, without a doubt, lived in the young part of the city with three other equally self-involved roommates—all guys from his fraternity back in the glory days. They now nursed small coke addictions and lived for every Saturday with the boys, either golfing or watching "the big game." And if, just if, he happened to have any cultural awareness at all, it came from listening to a podcast hosted by an obnoxious, short man with a microphone and an inferiority complex. She'd met "Matt," before and she *wasn't* interested.

"Morgan Stanley?" asked Olivia, feigning surprise. Matt's eager nod ruined his attempt at nonchalance. "I love her clothes," gushed Olivia.

Matt stepped to the side to let a busboy pass through. "No, no," he said, leaning closer. "Morgan Stanley. Money." He rubbed his fingers together in a gesture like an Italian mobster.

"Yes! Morgan's clothes are expensive!" mocked Olivia in response, finding great joy in the misunderstanding she'd created. "But sometimes cheaper online. Especially the dresses."

"Banking!" he barked. "Finance. Investments!" He ran his hand through his hair, his eyes wild. "Morgan Stanley!" he shouted again.

A few people turned to stare. Olivia held her palms up weakly. "Sorry, I guess I'm just stupid?" she responded innocently. She took a few steps back before turning around and smirking.

The pink lights dimmed, casting a haze over the crowd. Olivia blinked her eyes as she scanned the U-shaped bar for Margot. She walked toward the plush couches and saw a glimmer of silver.

"There you are!" Olivia called.

Margot sat on the corner of the couch, drink resting on the glass table in front of her. Its rim touched the side of another glass directly next to it. Olivia's eyes followed the second drink to its owner, a man in a green button-down shirt. He smiled.

"Liv!" exclaimed Margot, looking up. "Come sit." Margot gestured to the free chair beside the couch. "There's someone I want you to meet." Olivia noticed the man in the green shirt's hand was intertwined with Margot's. She found this odd; Margot wasn't into public displays of affection. Those "made things too serious," to quote Margot.

Margot grinned and gestured to the man. "This is Ben."

Olivia's brain searched through its rolodex of "Bens."

"The real estate broker I told you about," added Margot, as if she was reading Olivia's mind.

"Oh!" acknowledged Olivia, trying to mask her surprise that Ben from November was still around.

"I wanted you two to meet!" explained Margot. She looked fondly at Ben. "So I told him to drop by. You don't mind, do you?"

Olivia watched Margot nestle her face into Ben's shoulder. The music pumped louder, the lights bounced off the disco balls, highlighting their smiles—as if Olivia couldn't see them clearly enough already.

"No, of course not!" lied Olivia. "Nice to meet you, Ben." She stuck out a hand, wondering if it was too late to apologize to Mr. Morgan Stanley. She felt guilty for her cruel trick.

After five minutes of watching Margot and Ben stare into each other's eyes, Olivia tossed back the rest of her drink and stood up. "It's getting pretty late. I think I'm gonna head out."

"Really?" asked Margot, without looking up.

"Yeah. It seems like girls' night is over."

She stood up and left before Margot could respond.

Olivia pushed open the bar door and breathed in the night air. It was nearly two. The red awning of a pizza shop across the street called her name. Olivia paid for a slice with the loose change in the bottom of her purse and sat alone on the curb with her greasy paper plate.

CHAPTER 12

Olivia awoke the following Friday morning thinking about Violet Jones. Not just as the first Black anchor of *Happy Hour*, but as the woman who made a career, a life for herself out of seemingly nothing. Born into a humble, single-parent family in Georgia, she bagged groceries while earning her GED and saved up enough money to put herself through college. Driving forty-five minutes north of Atlanta, she practiced news reports in the car, mimicking the radio anchors to prepare for class. She was always home in time for dinner with her father, Al. Then she fell in love with broadcasting. Upon graduation, she jumped on any news set that would have her, delivering scripts, fetching coffee, carrying gear or laying cables, even holding the boom mic, oftentimes working for free.

It was her love of journalism—her belief in the power of the right story landing in front of the right viewer and changing their life forever—that guided her track. She secured her first behind the desk job in Helen, Georgia, a town with a population of just over five hundred people, when she was twenty-three. She'd wake at five in the morning, do her own hair and makeup, and read through her scripts two full times before going to air at ten. She began writing her notes and interview questions in ballpoint pen on small notecards that she'd place on her lap just underneath the desk, always using blue ink. Her determination, work ethic, and sheer star power couldn't be contained, and slowly but surely, she made her way to network news. Not without two children, a divorce, and a very public custody scandal. Still, as she sat behind the Atlas desk, having moderated presidential debates, interviewed world leaders in their home countries like Russia and Japan, and won a Peabody Award, Violet and her belief in stories that needed to be told—to teach, humble, entertain, and delight viewers—acted as her guiding force. *How badass is that?*

Not to mention, she started it all without a single initial connection to the industry. No rich uncle or executive father pulled strings to get her in. Olivia liked that she and Violet had that in common. They did it all by themselves.

The snow came down unseasonably fast and heavy as Olivia readied herself for work. She searched through the hallway closet for snow boots and decided Gwen must have stolen them. *Or maybe they were Gwen's all along?* She thought of her sister as she stuck her feet into black flats instead (she didn't have the energy for heeled shoes anymore) and how they'd only exchanged texts since Olivia told her about her terrible night out with Margot.

There was so much more she wished to share with Gwen. So much she wanted Gwen to help her sort through and reason. Without her, Olivia's thoughts felt thick and scrambled. Like Smith's eggless egg salad. She hadn't lived in a world in which she couldn't confide in Gwen. It made her furious her sister wasn't trying harder to reach her. It was as if her promise to call every day meant nothing.

At 7:50 a.m., Olivia left the Control Room and power walked to the bathroom, passing by Justin Timberlake in his green room. As she hustled back, she spotted Wesley near the studio doors, the golden light spilling out into the hallway.

"Big day, Wesley!" she announced. "The debut of your first full story!"

"Thanks, Liv." He smiled. "My first human interest piece as a producer!" He nervously drummed his fingers against the clipboard in his hands. She noticed Wesley was extra dressed up today in a blue button-down and tweed blazer. "It's such a great interview, too. That little girl who started the chess club is a rockstar!" he exclaimed. "I'm glad I got to do this story on her. Everyone is going to love the joy she brings to that nursing home."

"I can't wait!" responded Olivia. "Your piece is airing right after Justin Timberlake and right before Natalie Lewis." She turned back towards the control room.

"Natalie Lewis," she heard Wesley mumble. She looked over her shoulder and caught him shaking his head. "No comment," he scoffed.

Olivia didn't know much about Natalie Lewis, other than she was the wife of the president of Atlas News, but Olivia nodded anyway. "See you for coffee after the show." She was relishing her last days as a production assistant before she made the switch to associate producer and would lose her blessed postshow break.

She returned to the Control Room and slipped into her chair, noticing she'd left her phone on her desk. Olivia flipped it over and saw two missed calls from Andrea and a text from Margot: "Ben made it official last night!" Olivia rolled her eyes and hastily turned the phone face down. Margot had chosen to ignore several of Olivia's previous messages before sharing this news.

"There you are!" Andrea huffed, before demanding, "Where were you?" The clock read 7:53 a.m.

"I went to the bathroom," Olivia answered.

Andrea turned her chair toward Olivia, lips pressed in a thin line. She narrowed her eyes. "Well, be quicker next time! I needed you!"

"What can I help with, Andrea?" she offered.

"I need you to go into the rundown and change the show's segments. Immediately." Olivia instantly began clicking through the folders. "We are cutting nursing home chess club and extending the segment with Natalie Lewis instead," continued Andrea.

Olivia's mouse hovered over the nursing home folder. "That author of the dog book—" Olivia started to ask before stopping herself. She was afraid her clarifying question would be viewed as insolence.

Before Andrea could respond, they were interrupted by the arrival of black leather shoes and an overwhelming scent of cedarwood cologne. A silver Piaget watch with a sapphire face hit Olivia on the shoulder as a man reached to pat Andrea on the back.

"Ho, ho!" a deep voice hummed. "How's my favorite show!"

Expensive shoes, shiny watch, tailored suit—Olivia hadn't met the man in person, but she knew who he was. It was all starting to make sense.

"Simon!" Andrea jumped up. She smoothed the flyaways around her bun. "Exciting day to have you in the Control Room! We are all set for your lovely wife!"

Olivia watched Pete sit up straighter, Ken roll down his sleeves. Simon Lewis usually graced the covers of *The Hollywood Reporter* or *Variety*, answering interview questions about "life as TV's top executive" and showing off his boat collection. By Olivia's observation, his life seemed to be pretty luxurious.

"That is amazing, Annie!" he chortled. "Who else is accompanying my charming Natalie on the show today?" Olivia tried to determine the brand of his shoes but after not recognizing the logo decided she was too poor to know.

"Oh, it's a great lineup!" answered Andrea, full of vigor Olivia had never seen before. "We've got Justin Timberlake, your wife's amazing book on vegan dog treats, of course, and then an investigative segment into Broadway's diversity behind the curtain!"

"Cut that last segment," Simon said curtly. "I have a few buddies producing on Broadway. That won't look good for them."

Olivia choked on a sip from her water bottle.

"Certainly, Simon." Andrea nodded. She tapped on Olivia's desk expectantly, making sure she got the note. Olivia clicked through the rundown.

"Great." Simon took a few steps back and entered the middle row of computers. "Ken, a quick word before air? There are some Nielsen ratings I'd like to discuss."

Ken and Simon disappeared into the hallway, leaving behind a trail of cedarwood lingering in the air. Olivia finished updating the rundown, moving out poor Wesley's segment and ditching the investigative piece on diversity. It seemed stories could only be aired when they benefited the president of Atlas News.

"Olivia, are you done yet?" prodded Andrea.

"Yes, Andrea it's—"

"Pete!" Andrea thundered. "I see *three* chairs behind Violet's desk. We only need two! Violet and Justin," she barked. "Who else are we expecting, Joey Fatone?"

Andrea flung her arms into the air, knocking over the cup of coffee on her desk. Brown liquid spilled across the gray surface. "Dammit! I don't have time for this!"

"Get the kid to clean it," dismissed Pete, glaring at Andrea.

The monitors went black. The lights cut out. The preshow chatter and buzz disappeared as if someone had pressed mute. Two spotlights appeared. One on Pete, one on Olivia. The rest of the room was frozen.

"Olivia!" declared in a voice she didn't recognize. A rumble grew from deep within her chest. "My name is Olivia!" She was on her feet before she knew what she was doing.

Olivia turned and bravely addressed the front row. "Pete, I have worked here for more than a year. You can call me Olivia." Her hands were trembling. Her heart was pounding. Not a single staffer looked up from their computer.

Pete raised an eyebrow in her direction then turned toward the large screens. "Okay gang, let's set for the top of the show in sixty seconds," he called through his headset.

Everyone continued working. Andrea spoke to Violet in her headset, the back row of staffers made their time checks and loaded the teleprompter. No one seemed to have noticed her outburst. It was like nothing had happened at all. Olivia sank into her chair, wordless for the duration of the show.

~

Later that evening Olivia unhappily took the subway home. She preferred the walk to clear her mind, but the snow was too deep and without snow boots the trek was impossible. She fed her card into the machine, which beeped back angrily at her. She tried again. The machine beeped a second time. *Insufficient fare*, it read. Sighing, she took her card over to the boxy metal machines and slipped her debit card into the slot. She was met with more angry beeps. *Card declined.* She fished a crumpled five-dollar bill from the bottom of her purse and tried not to cry. She couldn't ask her parents for money. She didn't want to face any more questions from her mother.

As Olivia rode the B train downtown, she wondered if it had been like this for Violet. If she had endured office politics and snippy comments and people forgetting her name. If she'd had a pit in her stomach every time she opened an email or sat down in a control room. How did Violet take it when she had no money in her bank account? What about her social life? When Violet was working her way up, did she have time to date or have fun? Or was everything outside her pursuit of becoming an anchor irrelevant?

Maybe Violet wasn't thrown by bad managers or early mornings. Maybe her belief in the power of journalism, the significance of breaking a story, was so strong it carried her past the obstacles in her way. As Olivia transferred to the R train at Herald Square, she realized that for herself, her passion for morning news and human interest stories wasn't enough. The joy that *Happy Hour* brought her as a viewer did not carry over as a staffer. Whatever fight to push through that had been in Violet was dwindling in Olivia.

The train bumped and jerked toward 14th Street, and Olivia made eye contact with a man in a long brown raincoat. He winked at her before pulling out a full cannoli from his pocket. She watched a chocolate chip fall to the floor.

It reminded her of the game she had with Margot where they tried to one-up each other with the crazy things they saw on the subway. She decided Margot must've had an off night on Saturday. She didn't want to be upset with her friend. Olivia pulled out her phone and responded to Margot's message from the morning.

"*That's great! Let's celebrate next week? Atlas gave out tickets to* Hamilton, *my treat.*"

Margot quickly responded back:

"*Ben and I already went. So good!*"

Olivia put her phone away until she reached her apartment.

With the gentle turn of her key, she dropped her bag on the floor and tossed her wallet and phone on the counter. She turned on the stove and filled a pot with water, dragging it onto the burner.

Olivia had just added the noodles when she noticed an incoming call from Gwen. Her pulse quickened. She didn't know if she was angry or sad or disappointed or a mixture of all those emotions, but she knew she wanted to speak with her sister.

"Gwen?" she asked tentatively.

"Hi Liv. I'm just getting back from a late dinner with Henry. How are you?"

Olivia hovered over the pot. *Who the fuck is Henry?*

CHAPTER 13

"Who's Henry?" asked Olivia coolly. Although it hardly sounded relaxed; her voice came out high-pitched and strained.

"He's my—well, he's my flatmate," responded Gwen slowly.

Olivia turned off the stove and abandoned her noodles. "Is that a roommate? I thought you were living alone," she remarked, walking over to the couch.

"I was going to, but—it's a long story," sighed Gwen.

Olivia sat down and ran her hands through her long hair. There was so much she wanted, needed, to talk to Gwen about. She was overwhelmed with where to begin.

"I bet, a lot has happened since we last talked," snipped Olivia.

"Don't get upset, Liv," said Gwen defensively. "We've been playing phone tag, it's no one's fault."

Well, I'm not the one who moved to London.

"So, who's Henry?" she repeated, glad Jess wasn't home so she could speak freely. She didn't need her hearing this bitchy side so early on. They were still in their initial impressions phase.

Gwen exhaled slowly. "He *is* my flatmate," she began. "Meredith knew him from uni at Georgetown. She gave him my number so he could show me around London, help me get settled, you know, just as a friend of a friend." Gwen's use of the word "uni" didn't sound as cute anymore.

"Anyway," she continued, "We got coffee a few times and he told me he had an open room in his flat. And when he offered it to me, I—I took it."

Olivia was surprised to hear Gwen sounding so nervous. "Cool," she responded. "So why are you being so weird?"

"We're sort of—I mean, I don't know how it happened," Gwen fumbled her words, "but we're kind of … dating now."

"Oh!" Olivia said in surprise. "That's great!" She feigned enthusiasm, studying her fingers, counting the weeks Gwen had been in London. Four? Give or take a few days. She leaned back on the couch; she was sensing a theme. "Well, now I get why we haven't spoken in days. Weeks actually. You're busy with Henry."

"That's not fair, Liv," Gwen responded, her voice still quiet and low.

"Look, I'd love to chat more," Olivia said, rising from the couch and re-entering the kitchen. "I actually would." She looked into the pot and saw her noodles had congealed. "But I have my annual Christmas party tonight at Lucy and Luke's and I have to shower."

"I remember that party," said Gwen. "Do you have to go? Will Scott be there?"

"Yes Gwen," snapped Olivia. "And yes he will, but these are *my* friends." She picked up a fork and stirred the soggy noodles. "I actually follow through on things when I say I'll do them."

There was silence as Olivia's words sank in.

"Okay, I understand," reasoned Gwen quietly. "Maybe we can talk tomorrow."

"Don't bother," hissed Olivia as she disconnected the call. "You'd probably have to check with Henry, anyway," she mumbled to herself, dumping her noodles into a bowl and carrying it into her room.

Olivia wasn't ready to face Scott but couldn't think of a good enough excuse to get out of this party. *Why is telling a lie more socially encouraged than just saying I don't want to go?* She'd played the old "stuck on the subway," or "mouse in my apartment," or "the police have surrounded my block in search of an escaped fugitive so I can't open my door" cards too many times when she was tired. In New York City almost anything could be an excuse, the more absurd the more believable. The only excuse that *didn't* work was she couldn't emotionally bear the burden of this social gathering. New Yorkers had thick skin, they were tough, and none of them wanted to be where they were half of the time anyway!

Besides, she had volunteered to bring wine and dessert and had already spent part of her paycheck purchasing cookie dough and Chianti. The longer Olivia thought about it, brushing through her hair and recurling the ends, the more she rationalized that this party was tradition. She wasn't going to ignore tradition just because of Scott. Her breath began to flow more evenly as she skimmed through the clothes in her closet. She was allowed to do what she wanted! And what she wanted was to wear a dark brown sweater dress because she liked it and not because it made her butt look extra good. *So there!*

~

Two hours and one smoke alarm later, Olivia knocked on the door of Lucy and Luke's Upper East Side apartment—a bottle of wine in one hand and a plate of cookies with burnt bottoms in the other. It was the third annual "Friends-mas" dinner party. The name wasn't great, but Drew had drunkenly shouted it one year and it had stuck around.

"Liv!" exclaimed Lucy as she opened the door. She looked glowy and petite in a bright red dress and little candy cane earrings. Her makeup was flawless, almost as if it was airbrushed. Olivia presented her with the cookies she'd baked, careful to hide the bottoms. "I'm glad you could make it! It's been too long!"

Had it really been that long since she'd last seen her friends? Olivia tried to think back to the last group gathering. Was it something around Thanksgiving, or maybe it had been Halloween?

Olivia smiled sheepishly as Lucy placed her cookies on a long folding table that had been erected in her living room. A paper tablecloth of cartoon snowmen covered its surface, with a smattering of Tupperware and trays of cheese, crackers, mini hotdogs, mashed potatoes, meatballs, even lasagna (*ambitious*, thought Olivia) sitting on top. Silver streamers decorated the walls, glittery snowflakes hung from the ceiling, poinsettias filled the windowsill, and a balloon arch framed the kitchen entrance. A keg sat in the corner next to a full-sized Christmas tree. Justin Bieber's "Mistletoe" played from the speakers.

"Wow, you really outdid yourself this year!" Olivia commented. Lucy beamed.

She noticed there was another plate of cookies already displayed on the table as she set down her wine. Olivia pursed her lips in dismay.

"Liv, the TV star!" Luke, in his Santa hat, welcomed her with a hug. "What's the story of the day?"

Olivia laughed. "Local girl burns cookies, avoids house fire," she reported. Luke patted her back.

"Hey, don't worry about it. Looks like someone else brought cookies anyway."

"I noticed," Olivia mumbled to her suede boots as Luke went to greet more friends at the door. She looked around the living room for Margot. Or rather, Margot *and* Ben. A long arm and a designer purse caught her eye, and she spotted them on the couch talking to Drew. She waved and walked toward them, having already decided she'd give the couple a fresh start.

"Drew, are you the Grinch?" she asked as she sat down next to Margot, noticing Drew was dressed in an outfit of all green.

"Only if you are a ho ho ho!" he quipped, grabbing his belly in a Santa-like gesture as he laughed.

Olivia rolled her eyes and playfully slapped him on the shoulder. "That doesn't even make sense!"

"If you must know, Olivia. I am actually mistletoe," he said, gesturing to his ensemble. "Care to test it out?" He closed his eyes and puckered his lips out towards her. Margot leaned over, picked a mini hotdog off her plate, and pressed it to his mouth instead. Drew opened his eyes widely in surprise. He laughed when he saw the snack and ate it in one bite. "Oh, pigs in a blanket, my one true love!" he cried with his mouth full. Margot and Olivia high-fived. Olivia took it as a good omen for the night.

She turned to address Ben, who didn't seem to find the exchange as amusing. "Welcome to Friends-mas, Ben." Olivia smiled politely.

"Thank you. I already feel far too sober for this party," he stated.

"Me too," she agreed. "Should we get a drink? I brought wine."

The three walked into the crowded kitchen, Olivia snagging her bottle on the way, and grabbed red solo cups from the counter. Just to the left of the refrigerator, she saw Evan, Jasmine, and a brown-haired girl in reindeer antlers she didn't recognize mixing vodka and Crystal Light. Jasmine and Evan were in matching elf sweaters.

Beyond them, just next to the window, was a head of perfectly styled ash brown hair.

Her breath caught in her throat.

Wearing a plain black sweater, a bottle of Blue Moon in hand, was Scott.

She had tried to prepare for this moment but still felt her heart fall to the bottom of her boots. She looked over to Margot but saw she was in deep conversation with Ben, their faces inches apart as they laughed. She couldn't handle Scott on her own, or at least not without several drinks first. Olivia turned her back to the window and walked out of the kitchen as quickly as her full cup of wine allowed.

"It looks like everyone's here," announced Lucy several moments later, snaking an arm around Luke's waist. He kissed the top of her head. "Shall we all sit down?" She gestured to the long table.

Margot and Ben emerged from the kitchen first and took the seats at the nearest end of the table. Olivia sat next to them. Jasmine and Evan joined after, filling the chairs toward the center.

"Scott and Olivia, you can sit over here," called Lucy. She pulled out two chairs at the far end of the table. Olivia looked up in confusion.

Maybe Lucy didn't know about their sort of breakup. She had assumed the whole group did at this point. In total honesty, Olivia had hoped they'd take her side and uninvite Scott after the way he strung her along.

She tried to catch Lucy's eye when she saw Scott walk out of the kitchen closely trailed by the brown-haired girl in antlers. "Olivia," Lucy called again when she saw them. "Down here!" she gestured to the empty chairs.

The scene began to move in slow motion. Olivia watched in horror as Scott and Antlers took the seats from Lucy, smiling at each other as they sat down. If this were a movie, a dark symphony would begin to build in the background. The brass instruments low and ominous, yet the strings sharp and high pitched, foreshadowing impending doom. The camera would zoom in on a close-up of Scott's smile before revealing the woman to his left. The symphony growing louder and louder until—

"Olivia and Olivia," exclaimed Drew. "Hey, now we have two!"

If Olivia's heart had already fallen into her boots, it had now sunk beneath the paneled wooden floors. She wished the rest of her body could crawl down there with it. She looked to Margot whose gaze was down at her empty plate.

"Ah, right I forgot," said Scott awkwardly, running a hand through his hair. "Some of you guys met her on Thursday, but this is—"

The symphony returned louder. Olivia watched the cartoon snowmen on the tablecloth join hands and begin to chant like a cursed choir. They shook and swayed, their eyes wide with fear. *Don't*, thought Olivia. *Don't say—*

Scott grinned. "—My girlfriend, Olivia."

A sinkhole cracked the table clean down the middle all the way to the center of the earth. Hot lava bubbled up from below and covered the meatballs, the lasagna, the mini hot-dogs. "Girlfriend!" taunted the snowmen as they began to twist together. "Girlfriend! Girlfriend!" They moved faster and faster until they blended into one vortex, sucking the table and all its food down into the fiery pit. Lava flames shot out one by one, burning the couch, the TV, the Christmas tree. Olivia watched in horror as Drew was struck by molten goo and melted before her eyes. She blinked and blinked but all she saw were smoke and flames. This was the end. She was sure of it.

The only object unmoving was the wine directly in front of Olivia. She grabbed for it like she was Frodo and it was the Ring. She swallowed a heavy gulp. It left a burning sensation in her stomach, which at least assuaged the pit of anguish and stopped the room from spinning.

"Hi everyone," greeted Other Olivia. "Thanks for having me!" She smiled warmly at Lucy.

The apocalyptic hole may have disappeared, but Olivia was still in agony. She set her face to stone, a habit she'd perfected thanks to *Happy Hour*. She could feel her friends looking at her.

"You guys kinda look alike!" announced Drew from the far end of the table. He had mashed potato on his chin.

"You're on a roll tonight, Drew," muttered Scott.

Olivia nudged Margot, who was still staring down at her plate. She didn't look up.

"You know who *you* kinda look like Drew?" quipped Evan. "That girl you brought home Thursday night!" he roared. Luke and Scott joined his laughter. "A major stain on your résumé, bro!"

Drew ducked his head and covered his red ears. "We didn't do anything! I was so drunk!" he whimpered.

"Man, even your fantasy league this season looked better," added Luke.

"And he—" Evan was wheezing he was laughing so hard. "He f—finished last!" He now had tears streaming down his face. "Oh man!"

Jasmine and Lucy giggled at their silly boyfriends. Olivia felt the urge to slap them.

She nudged Margot again. "Did you know about this?" she whispered, hurt seeping into her voice. Margot only stared back.

Had everyone known but her? She shifted her gaze ever so slowly down the table until Other Olivia came into view. Brown hair, seemingly similar height, besides that, there wasn't much they had in common. Olivia could think of no other words to describe the girl other than "normal." So, what did this Olivia have that she did not?

Her eyes strayed farther to the left until they found Scott. She noticed he was looking back. It was the first time they'd locked eyes all night. Olivia was overcome by a wave of nausea.

"Olivia, I'm dying to try your lasagna," said Lucy, breaking the silence that had fallen over the group. Real Olivia looked up at the mention of her name.

"I wasn't sure what to bring," confessed Other Olivia. "I hope it's okay. I brought cookies too, just in case."

"It's more than okay!" mused Lucy.

Olivia turned toward Margot. "What a try-hard with the lasagna," she whispered.

Margot shifted uncomfortably in her folding chair, finally meeting Olivia's eyes. "I don't know, it looks good," she reasoned, pulling the lasagna tray towards her.

"Thanks for the tip to add basil, Margot," Other Olivia called from her end of the table.

"Of course!" Margot responded sweetly. "I learned it from Scusi's on 56th Street." She cut a tiny square for Ben and then one for herself. Olivia watched in bewilderment as she and Ben fed each other bites. *Since when does Margot share cooking tips?*

"I love that restaurant!" exclaimed Lucy. "We should all go on a triple date there!"

Olivia aggressively put a full meatball in her mouth to stop herself from groaning. It appeared Margot was too busy to respond to her texts but somehow had time for "triple dates."

"Hey, Scott," said Luke loudly. "Your traps are looking big. You hittin' the gym?" he asked through a mouthful of cheese.

Olivia finished chewing and turned toward Margot once again. "Margot, how do you know her?" She was terse, fighting to keep her voice low. Thankfully the boys had begun shouting their gym routines across the table.

Margot and Ben shared a look. Olivia and Margot used to share looks. "I met her on Thursday," she explained quietly. "She's nice. You'd like her."

Olivia wanted to slap Margot, too. Her stomach churned so deeply she thought she was going to get sick at the table. "D—did everyone hang out on Thursday without me?" she stammered.

Olivia used to think her biggest fear was dying alone. Or maybe falling into one of those trapdoors on the sidewalk that led into the basement of most street-side shops. Or toilet snakes. She realized only then she had an even greater fear: being left behind. To think her friends had formed another group text without her left a burn in her heart so deep she thought it'd catch fire. It seemed everyone was leaving her behind these days.

"It was nothing Olivia, just after-work drinks," Margot said in a hushed voice. "We didn't invite you because we knew you wouldn't be able to make it with your schedule. Honestly, it was nothing."

"What the fuck, Margot," choked Olivia. She placed her napkin on her plate. "I'm going to be sick."

"Olivia, stop," pleaded Margot. "You're overreacting!"

She felt bile rising in her throat. "I would never." She took a deep breath, closing her eyes. "Never. Keep something like this from you." She trembled.

Margot put her fork down and huffed, "Olivia, there are no sides. We're all friends." She and Ben exchanged another look.

"I'm really going to be sick," Olivia said again. She rose from her chair and briskly moved toward the hallway bathroom.

In a series of rapid movements, she flicked on the light, locked the door, and vomited into the sink.

Everyone was moving on. They were living without her. Scott, Margot, Gwen, people who—until very recently—Olivia thought were closest to her, who really knew her and cared for her. Who had her best interests in mind and thought of her daily, the way she thought of them. They had all replaced her. That was it: she was replaceable. Forgettable. Left behind. Unlovable.

She sat on the toilet lid, one wall away from Scott's new Olivia, furious with Margot, let down by Gwen, distant from her parents, sapped from work, with no savings and nothing on the precipice besides a Christmas without her sister.

A knock on the door interrupted her sulking. She let out a sigh of relief. At last Margot still cared enough to check on her.

"Yo I gotta make holy water, hurry up," called Drew.

WINTER

CHAPTER 14

New York City turned especially gray in February. Not just from the low-hanging clouds that reflected onto the tall, windowed skyscrapers, but from the exhaust that pumped from the subway grates, the whitewashed grime that coated the taxis, the color of the slushy snow between the road and the sidewalk that never seemed to melt. The color of hats and scarves and mittens, the little line of sludge that formed on the toe of every shoe, even the skin tone of those not fortunate enough to head to Miami with the rest of the NYC elite.

The inside of Edit Room #5 was gray. Olivia had been staring at its walls for the past month after assuming her role as associate producer at the turn of the new year.

Each day she would arrive at the tiny room at exactly 3:55 a.m. to an inbox full of emails and a head full of increasing doubt. It was just her and the video editor inside the dark room. Olivia dictated the exact clips, sound bites, and images she wanted as the editor zipped away, piecing it all together. She'd work for nearly four hours straight, nose to the computer, without pausing for a bathroom break or even a sip of water. Each morning the cycle repeated; she'd even started to feel gray.

And each night she grew increasingly more exhausted. She'd hadn't spoken to Margot since Friends-mas or even considered seeing any of her other friends.

She'd also been in a stalemate with her mother, steadily declining her calls after their fight on Christmas morning. Olivia had made the family late for their annual holiday brunch. "Why did you have to sleep in, Olivia!" her mother complained, sitting on the couch fully dressed as Olivia entered the living room in her PJs.

"Maybe you'd understand why I'm so exhausted if you gave a *single* shit about my life!" Olivia had shrieked back. "Stop pretending you care!" The yell had sent her poor dog, Charlie, running under the family's kitchen table.

"We do not yell in this house!" her father had shouted back.

To round out her exhaustion, Andrea had taken to emailing and texting Olivia several times an evening, piling on to-dos for the next day.

"Don't forget to add the background music tomorrow."

"Reach out for a quote from the senator now so you'll have it by the morning."

It made Olivia feel tense. Constantly on edge. Just about anything seemed to faze her. "Have a good night, Olivia!" Jess had called from the hallway one evening. "I'm leaving for my date!"

Olivia had crawled into her bed and cried. When would *she* ever have time to go on dates?

~

On the first Friday in February, Olivia awoke with a stomachache.

She tried to ignore it as she worked on three different stories: a preview of the upcoming Winter Olympics, an overview on the Supreme Court's latest hearing, and an exploratory piece on Punxsutawney Phil, the world-famous Pennsylvanian groundhog. After all, it *was* Groundhog Day.

By the time her video editor sent the stories to Andrea for approval, Olivia's head had an ache to match her stomach. She fished around in her bag for an Advil but noticed the pill bottle was empty.

The edit room phone rang.

"Well, did he see his shadow?" she heard on the line, the slight Jersey accent lingering on the last word.

"It hasn't been released yet, Andrea." Olivia responded, confident she had checked the latest reports. The sun hadn't even risen yet.

"Olivia," Andrea sighed. "We *always* know ahead of time if he sees his shadow or not. Who do you think we are, the general population?" She snorted. "Call his people and update that video *now*." The phone line went dead.

Panic swelled in Olivia's chest. "Call his people?" It wasn't like there was a section in the Atlas directory for famous rodents.

She desperately texted Wesley, as she found herself so often doing.

"Ever call Punxsutawney Phil?"

She saw an incoming call from Gwen and angrily silenced it. Had she forgotten Olivia was *working*?

Wesley responded immediately.

"Yes actually, you'll want his handler. I think I have her number saved, one sec."

Olivia let out a sigh of relief and wiped the sweat above her upper lip. *Why is the room so hot today?* Wesley sent through the number and she typed back a heart, immediately calling the contact from her cell phone. The edit room phone rang again.

She answered it with her free hand and held it to her other ear. The editor raised an eyebrow as he saw Olivia with a different phone to each ear.

"Do you have it yet?" Andrea demanded.

"No, not yet—" Olivia said quickly.

"This isn't rocket science! We're talking about a *groundhog* for God's sake."

The other line continued to ring from her cell phone. Olivia's head was pounding, her throat felt like sandpaper, and she was so nauseous she thought about dragging in the trash can from the hallway.

The line in her left hand went dead while her cell phone was finally answered by a woman who referred to herself as Punxsutawney Phil's "agent." She assured Olivia that Phil would indeed be seeing his shadow that morning, signaling six more weeks of winter. *Just what we all need*, thought Olivia. *More gray.*

She raced to update the video and sent a fresh version to Andrea with ten minutes to air. As she rose from her chair with the intent to visit the water fountain, the edit room phone rang again.

"Violet doesn't have her notecards. The new PA messed up. I need you to fix it," Andrea ordered in one long breath before hanging up.

Olivia closed her eyes and pressed her lips together. They had gone through two new production assistants in January; both had been asked to leave before they were even fully trained. Andrea had called them "soft" and "slow," saying, "They'll never make it in this industry."

Olivia turned and practically ran to the elevator bank. She knew it wasn't her job, but if Violet's notecards were off, Violet was off. She couldn't bear to see Violet make a mistake.

There was no time to waste as she cut through the hallway, the pain in her stomach building with every step. The clock on her phone changed to 7:53 a.m. Another incoming call came from Gwen. Olivia ignored it.

She arrived at the nearly empty office to find a young-looking girl hunched over the printer and crying. "Here," Olivia offered, as she began pressing buttons on the printer. "Let me help you," she said softly. She had a feeling this girl wouldn't be around much longer either.

The girl pulled torn notecards out of the printer's mouth as more tears streamed down her face. Olivia tapped through the printer settings and grabbed a fresh stack of cards. The clock on the wall clicked to 7:55 a.m.

As they waited for the new notecards to print, Olivia noticed the girl was wearing a very tight pinstriped dress and inappropriately high heels for such a movement-intensive role. The clock clicked to 7:56 a.m.

Even if they delivered Violet's cards in time, there was no way she'd be able to make her notes or highlights. Why hadn't Andrea alerted Olivia sooner? The time changed to 7:57 a.m. and Olivia figured notecards with no notes were better than no notecards at all.

Still, the elevator was too far away, the studio hallway was too long. They'd never make it in time. Olivia whipped out her phone, formulating a plan as the line rang. "Stand at the bottom of the east stairs in thirty seconds!" she bellowed before hanging up. The last notecard shot out from the printer and she hastily tugged a rubber band around the stack and ran to the hallway. The young girl in her heels struggled to keep up. Olivia turned right, pushed open the emergency stair doors and ran to the railing. There, two flights down below, she saw a small blonde head look up. "Hallie! Catch!" She dropped the cards straight down the center rails. She heard the thud of the cardstock hit Hallie's hands and watched her friend disappear into the studio hallway.

Olivia returned to the office and stared at the TV monitor next to Andrea's door. There on the screen she saw the white marble desk, notecards in position. A wave of great relief washed over Olivia. A wave so strong she felt lightheaded. In fact, she turned around thinking she'd finally get some water when everything went to black.

CHAPTER 15

Something was very wrong. Olivia was in the fetal position, the side of her face pressed against the gray carpet of the office. She could smell its dirt. She lifted her head and noticed a high heel, the hem of a pinstriped dress.

"Are you okay?" the young girl asked, crouching down low. Her face was tear stained and her eyes were red. Behind her appeared a pink jacket, a flash of blonde hair. Hallie.

"Liv," said Hallie gently, patting her arm, "are you okay?"

"I—I didn't know what to do," the new production assistant explained nervously. "So I called the last number in your phone."

Olivia gave a weak smile. "Thanks. Is the show over?" she asked, blinking as the sharp lights hit her eyes.

Hallie shook her head. "No, we're in commercial break. I don't think you were out for more than a few seconds before Irene called me."

Olivia nodded and closed her eyes. The pain in her stomach had returned. It was burning, radiating to her back. She'd never felt this sick before. *This promotion is literally going to kill me.* And yet, she still pictured Andrea calling an empty edit room, the seat beside her in the Control Room empty. The show was on the air; they couldn't all be here in the office.

Olivia looked at Hallie. "You guys should go back. I think—I think I have to go to the hospital."

Hallie's eyes widened. "Should I call an ambulance?"

"No, no. I can't afford it," dismissed Olivia.

"I'll call an Uber," reasoned Hallie.

"Traffic will be awful right now," Olivia complained.

"Do you want to go to the hospital or not?" asked Hallie.

Olivia gave a weak laugh. She slowly pushed herself up to her feet and took a few tentative steps.

"I—I think I can take the train," she reasoned. "It goes right to the NYU hospital."

Maybe Margot could meet her there so she wouldn't be alone. Jess was away with friends in the Catskills. Olivia didn't really *want* to see Margot, but she didn't have anyone else nearby to call. Hallie watched her carefully as Olivia reached for her phone on the floor and dialed. There was no answer on the line. "I guess I'm gonna take the train now then." Olivia fumbled with her words.

"*We'll* take the train," Hallie corrected. "I'm coming with you." She turned to Irene and lightly touched her arm. "Can you go back to the Control Room and explain to Andrea where we are?" Irene nodded and took off down the hall as fast as her heels allowed.

"You don't have to come," said Olivia quietly, another wave of nausea sending her back down to her knees.

"Yes I do," she stated. "Violet has what she needs for the show. She'll be okay without me. Let me just grab a few things." She looked down at Olivia, who had moved to hug the nearby trash can. "Don't go anywhere," she directed. Olivia laughed feebly despite the pain.

Hallie hurried down the hall. Olivia looked up from the bottom of the bin to find herself staring directly at the glass door of Andrea's empty office. *God, if I'm dying, please don't let this be the last thing I see*, she prayed. She had a feeling that even after death Andrea would make her come into work the next day.

Three minutes later, Hallie reappeared holding Olivia's coat and bag, a bottle of water, saltine crackers, and a stuffed teddy bear. The gesture was so sweet it brought tears to Olivia's eyes.

"Someone sent this to Violet," explained Hallie holding up the fuzzy brown bear. "But I thought you needed it more," she reasoned, passing the bear to Olivia who hugged its soft fur tightly.

"It's already helping," Olivia sniffed.

"I'm glad," laughed Hallie. "Just don't throw up on it."

She helped Olivia to her feet and draped her coat over her shoulders. Together they made their way to the elevator bank, out the lobby, and across the street to the subway station. Every few yards felt like a mile. Olivia took tiny steps, Hallie holding her arm as if she was a toddler. In a way, it reminded Olivia of when she *was* that much younger. Helpless, dependent on her parents, unable to do anything for herself. Nowadays, she felt like she did *everything* for herself: cooking, cleaning, paying bills, killing bugs—she forgot what it was like to really rely on someone. It seemed like Gwen had been gone for years.

They stepped onto the subway platform with the train mercifully appearing within seconds. "Here." Hallie handed her a plastic baggie. "Just in case. Sometimes the smells on the train make *me* want to vomit." Olivia clutched the teddy bear as they sat down, willing herself at every bump to not get sick.

Hallie reassuringly patted her back when they finally checked into the emergency room. It looked relatively empty as they took seats on the blue cushioned chairs and waited for Olivia's name to be called. Olivia cradled her knees to her chest and closed her eyes, holding the bear against her stomach. Hallie swiped through her emails, occasionally offering water or a saltine as time passed.

Olivia's phone buzzed in her pocket. Another call from Gwen.

Her fingers trembled as she answered it this time. "Gwen," she whispered.

"Olivia. Please stop ignoring me—"

"Gwen," repeated Olivia, realizing how comforting it felt to hear her sister's voice. "I'm at the hospital. I don't really have time to talk."

"What? Are you okay? What's going on?"

Olivia hugged her knees tighter. "I don't know, they're about to call me back," she answered. "Hallie's with me. Can you tell Mom and Dad?"

She heard Gwen take in a sharp breath. "You haven't called them yet?"

"Please, Gwen—"

"Olivia?" a nurse appeared in the doorway. Hallie tapped her arm.

"I gotta go. Love you." Olivia hung up and slowly rose to her feet. Hallie was already holding her coat and bag.

It was only then, as they walked deeper into the hospital, that Olivia felt scared. She wished she was back at the show. She wished it was just a normal morning. She wished her stomach would, just for one millisecond, stop hurting. She wished her parents were there.

CHAPTER 16

Olivia awoke to a pair of hazel eyes staring into hers. Brown in the center and gold along the edges.

"Mom," she croaked. She began to cry.

Her mother leaned over the edge of the hospital bed and hugged Olivia tightly. "The doctor said you can go home now."

She briefly tore her eyes away from her mom's face and noticed a small suitcase in the corner. The sky was dark through the room's slim window.

"When did you get in?" Olivia asked.

"About four hours ago," her mother replied, pushing the hair off Olivia's forehead. "You've been sleeping for a while, and I didn't want to wake you," she explained quietly. "I got on the first flight after Gwen called me." She handed Olivia a tissue. There was no underlying jab to her comment, no bite that could have so easily been attributed to Olivia not answering her calls. Her tone was warm, soothing.

Olivia wiped her eyes. She felt tired, but comforted, safe, relieved. She wasn't alone anymore.

A bump under the blankets caught her eye, and she pulled back the sheets to reveal the teddy bear Hallie had given her. Olivia smiled.

Earlier that afternoon, after a series of tests, the doctors had diagnosed Olivia with dehydration, which explained the fainting and vomiting, and an ulcer, which explained her stomach pain. She thought those were only for old people.

"Can you check me for one too?" Hallie had asked, grabbing her coat. "We have the same job, so it'd only make sense."

The doctor chuckled and recommended they both try to lighten their stress. The fluids and rest already had Olivia feeling much better, and the doctor assured her that antibiotics could heal her ulcer. "I'd lay off the coffees for a long while, too," he'd suggested.

No matter how many times Olivia thanked Hallie, it didn't feel like enough.

Olivia grabbed the teddy bear and held it close to her chest while her mom rolled her suitcase to the door.

"Ready, honey?" she asked quietly.

Twenty minutes later, they stood outside the hospital waiting for a taxi. The background of the city against her mother looked out of place. She was used to seeing her mother's soft features against the mowed grass and clean sidewalks of suburbia. The tall buildings and long blocks made her look small and fragile. Olivia felt an overwhelming desire to shield her mom from the speeding taxis, the trash on the streets, the shouting in the alleyways.

Once they were back to Olivia's apartment, she took a shower while her mom changed her sheets. She then crawled into bed, her mom draping an extra blanket over her legs. "Are you in pain?" she asked as she began to rub the bottoms of her daughter's feet. Olivia shook her head.

The gentle touch of her mother's hands reminded her of the last time Margot did her makeup. And of the last time

Gwen pulled her into a hug. Of the soft comfort of Scott's hand intertwined with hers, and the way Hallie had helped her onto the train. It was the touch of someone showing they cared. It brought tears to her eyes.

Maybe her mom didn't understand television. Maybe her mom was quick to judge, strong minded, and convinced that Olivia should be making more money, working for a better manager. Maybe she just wanted the best for her.

Olivia felt a pang of sadness, knowing she had pushed her mom away. She'd been relying too heavily on her faith in television to prove her wrong.

Olivia watched her mom lovingly rub her feet and felt like the most ungrateful daughter in the world. "My stomach doesn't hurt," answered Olivia. "B—but." She felt the tears fall fast and heavy. She blamed the painkillers for making her so blubbery and emotional. "But I still feel so bad," she cried.

Her heart ached for all the things she had loved and lost over the past half year.

Her mom moved closer to her on the bed, tucking a strand of hair behind Olivia's ear. "You were really working yourself to the bone, poor thing, weren't you?" she said softly.

Olivia nodded. "I don't know what I'm doing anymore," she sobbed. She took a deep inhale. "And—and everyone else seems to be doing great." She wiped her face with the back of her hand.

Her mother shook her head and pulled the blanket up higher around Olivia's shoulders. "I'm sure that's not true."

"It is!" Olivia cried. "Gwen got this big promotion, and moved to London and met ... *Henry,*" she emphasized. "And Margot's living on her own and she's now with *Ben*!" Her mother patted her arm soothingly, as the tears fell. "I thought I was getting it right, but I'm not!"

The effort Olivia put into her job, her friendships, her relationships—it didn't seem like it moved her forward at all. Why was it so much easier for the people around her?

"Maybe you're a little jealous they have boyfriends?" her mom offered.

Olivia shook her head. "I am *not* jealous." She sniffed defensively. "I'm happy for them. I am. It's possible to be happy for someone and feel left behind at the same time," she said, wiping another tear with her hand. Her mother reached into her pocket and handed her a tissue.

Olivia took another deep breath. "I feel like for Gwen, and Margot especially, they stopped needing me—" She wiped her nose as she thought of the right words. "They're gone, they left— they—" she hiccupped. "They went to Boy-friend Island!" she finally decided.

Her mother furrowed her brow. "What's Boyfriend Island?"

"I don't know, I just made it up!" cried Olivia. She pictured Gwen and Margot on a tropical island in grass skirts surrounded by shrimp cocktails and piña coladas. Henry and Ben sat next to them wearing Hawaiian shirts, surrounded by fluttering doves feeding them grapes off the vine. "Lovebirds Only," read a wooden sign in the sand. There was a bubble around the whole island, like a huge bright pink Bazooka gum bubble. Olivia couldn't get in no matter how hard she pushed from the water's edge.

The painkillers must have really set in.

Her mother's mouth curled into a smile, as if she could see the image in Olivia's mind. "You always were very imaginative, Livvy," she laughed. Olivia wiped at the tears on her face.

"So, they aren't allowed to enjoy their boyfriends?" she continued slowly, looking up at her daughter. "That seems a little selfish, no?"

"You don't have to stay the night, you know," retorted Olivia, pouting her lips.

Her mother laughed again. "I understand what you're saying Olivia, I'm just trying to show you it's not always all about you."

"Yes, it is." Olivia sniffed again. Her face broke into a smile as she gave her mom a small wink.

Her mother chuckled and resumed rubbing Olivia's arm. They stayed like that for some time, Olivia enjoying the comforting touch of her mother's fingertips, the quiet of the apartment.

"If I can tell you anything," her mother finally said. "It's that your twenties are like this. Everyone has something that you want and sometimes it just isn't fun." She cleared her throat and sat up straighter. "I had friends go to Boyfriend Island, too." She smiled. "And they do come back, you know. You have to be patient and let them enjoy their vacation, and hope that they're patient when *you* eventually go to Boyfriend Island."

Olivia nodded as thin tears watered her cheeks again. She petted the teddy bear in her arms.

"I'm sorry I don't call you more," said Olivia.

She watched the corners of her mom's eyes wrinkle, her bottom lip slightly jut out. Her mom took a quick, uneven breath and said, "I can be helpful sometimes, right?"

She then reached over and patted the little brown bear in Olivia's arms. Her hazel eyes magnified with tears. "You can always talk to me," she said. "Whenever you call, I'll always answer."

~

The night before her first day back at work, Olivia sat in her shower and cried. It went against everything the doctors told her to do in terms of managing her stress, but she couldn't help it. She let the hot water run over her body and willed herself to find the strength to wake up at three in the morning again. The weekend off, plus Monday, had Olivia feeling the best she'd felt in a long time. She'd slept in late, binged old Netflix shows she'd never gotten around to watching, and took pleasant walks up and down her street with her mom. She cried when her mom went back to North Carolina early Monday afternoon.

Olivia did everything she could to make her return feel more bearable. She'd laid out her clothes the night before, packed her favorite sandwich for lunch, and arrived at Atlas extra early to give herself time to adjust and fill her water bottle.

She made it through the morning with fewer calls than expected from Andrea. The stories she cut with her editor only required minor changes. There were no crazy hunts or interview subjects she had to chase. It actually seemed okay. Maybe she had been making things feel worse than they really were. Perhaps the short break was all she needed.

After the show, Wesley and Hallie walked over to her desk in the office and presented her with flowers and an "I heart NYC" shirt signed by her favorite D-list celebrity.

"Brad Bradley from *Summer Season*?" she cried. "You guys!"

Wesley and Hallie smiled proudly. "He was a guest yesterday," informed Hallie. "It was Wesley who remembered that you *love* him."

"But it was Hallie who asked him to sign the shirt." Wesley winked.

Olivia laughed and clutched the shirt to her chest. "I really don't know what I would do without you two. This really means so much." She smiled. "I mean, he's just *so* hot."

Her friends laughed with her and her smile grew wider. These moments made her feel strong, like her struggle in the industry was worth it. That if she pushed through, she could have everything she wanted.

At the other end of the office, Olivia saw a cardigan-wrapped Andrea emerge from behind her glass door. She walked towards Olivia's chair. Wesley and Hallie slipped back to their seats.

"So Olivia, how was your vacation?" asked Andrea, tapping on Olivia's desk with her pen.

Olivia was so stunned she couldn't open her mouth. Her brain couldn't think of a sentence. They had emailed back and forth about her absence over the weekend. Surely Andrea was joking. She'd even said to Olivia, "Feel better, but when will you be back?" which Olivia considered to be as close to sympathy as Andrea's heart could allow.

Andrea took Olivia's silence as a response. "Look," she continued, eyeing the T-shirt in Olivia's hands, "the night associate producer just called in sick."

Olivia held her breath.

"So, I need you to work a double shift tonight."

CHAPTER 17

She expected the stacks of scripts to flurry and shred themselves into a million pieces, falling down like heavy rain. The big monitor to rip from the walls and thunder as it cartwheeled down the hall. The computers to spark and implode, shooting like lightning across the office. She braced herself, waiting for the *Happy Hour* mugs that lined producers' desks to smash and whirl into a tornado, whizzing by Andrea and cutting her bun clean off.

Several times she blinked, waiting for the cataclysmic event.

But it never came.

Instead, Olivia felt a storm rising inside herself. An urgency as the tides within her swelled and her thoughts crested like waves. She'd capsize if she didn't address it, this unsettling pull. This unrest that traveled from her temple down to her navel to the back of her knees.

Andrea turned back to her office. Olivia waited for the glass door to close before leaping out of her chair. She didn't dare look at Hallie or Wesley; they had done all they could anyway.

Her feet moved briskly toward the elevator, determined to lead her exactly where she knew she had to go. If they didn't act quickly enough, she would reconsider. Change her mind. She urged them to walk faster.

There were so many moments for which she wished she had more time. More time with Gwen, more time in the edit room, more time recovering at home with her mom. For once, she didn't want more time. In this moment, she'd had enough.

Olivia arrived at the eleventh floor and stared straight ahead. With her chest proud and shoulders back, she carried herself like someone who mattered. As someone worthy of respect, care, and admiration.

The floor was mostly office space. No studio gear, no warm LED lights. Olivia wound her way through the cubicles, largely ignored by the workers at their desks. She headed towards the glass office doors that lined the back walls. It had to be one of these. She slowed her feet, allowing herself to read each name etched outside the doors.

"Are you looking for someone?" A young man in a cubicle popped his head just over the barrier.

Olivia kept her eyes focused on the office doors and continued walking. Her face lit up when she saw the name outside: "Mary Catherine Johnson, News HR." There she was.

"I found her," said Olivia without turning her head.

She knocked briskly on the door two times before turning the handle.

"You can't just walk in—" he whined.

Mary looked up from her desk. Olivia heard music playing through the computer speakers. She watched as Mary fumbled to turn it off, clearly startled by the interruption. Mary had probably never participated in a last minute, impromptu meeting in her life.

"Oh my, what a surprise!" she exclaimed. She wiggled on her seat behind a brown wooden desk, adjusting her cardigan and pushing her glasses up the bridge of her nose. Olivia smiled politely, taking in the large office. The walls were a yellow-white, like fungus, the carpet a light brown like dirt.

"Mary, do you have a moment?" Olivia asked gently, trying to hide her distress. The storm inside had grown, the winds quickened, the chaos dangerously close to swallowing her whole. She helped herself to an armchair across from the desk, determined to keep it at bay.

Mary looked at her with wide eyes. She shuffled a stack of papers, squabbling about a meeting she had to attend in thirty minutes.

"This won't take long," Olivia assured.

Mary nodded and removed her glasses and set them on the desk. She looked up and leaned forward.

Olivia took a deep breath. In that instant a highlight reel played millisecond flashes of her time at *Happy Hour*: The egg on the screen, Andrea's spilled coffee, the cream cheese-stained blouse, the snakelike eyes of Simon Lewis, his tongue slithering across the camera lens. The reel played on, showing a snapshot of Olivia's bank account, Gwen's boxes piled high in their hallway, a hospital bed, Margot and Other Olivia exchanging a smile.

Olivia blinked and exhaled slowly, the tape went to black, the room came back into focus. The storm on the edge of her lips.

Her eyes stared into Mary's with unwavering confidence.

"Mary, I'd like to respectfully quit *Happy Hour*."

She watched the rest of the conversation unfold as an out-of-body experience. She drifted to the top of Mary's corner shelving unit, looking down at a girl she never thought she'd become.

"But you were just promoted!" Mary reasoned.

"Yes, and I am very appreciative, but I feel strongly about this decision," Olivia affirmed, her words clear and focused. She waited for Mary's counter. Maybe she would try to win her over with more money? Promise better hours? Olivia's mind was made, but it wouldn't hurt to hear how badly they wanted her to stay.

"Well if you're leaving for a competing network I'll call you an exit car now," sighed Mary. "Someone else will clean out your desk." She turned and began typing.

Olivia watched her own face turn white. After all that time, the early mornings, the long hours, she'd be escorted out of Atlas like a fugitive?

"No, Mary," quickly interrupted Olivia. "I'm not going to another network. I'm just leaving." She paused. "For myself."

Mary nodded and accepted her resignation, albeit flabbergasted Olivia hadn't set up a formal termination meeting. She explained Olivia still needed to finish out her two weeks, as per company policy. Olivia agreed, already feeling lighter.

Olivia came back into her body as she stood and exited Mary's office. The storm had settled inside her.

CHAPTER 18

"The little guy was stuck in the marsh. I saw 'em, just tryna claw his way out, but the brambles had 'em pretty good."

"And that's where you came in?" asked Violet, the sun flashing across the lens.

"Righto. I hopped in that ol' water, cleared the debris. Set that gator free!" sang Gator Guy. "Gator done baby!"

Olivia rewound the tape. The monitor skipped to the beginning of the interview, showing Violet walking across the Florida Everglades in bright yellow galoshes and a white sun hat. The colors popped against her dark skin.

The clock struck 2:00 a.m. in Edit Room #5. Olivia had just finished her edits on an Atlas cross-promotional interview between Violet and Gator Guy. After the director yelled cut, the tape had continued to role and she heard Gator Guy say in a thick Boston accent, "That gatah was wicked tangled." She was devastated, but hardly surprised, to learn his southern charm was fake. She decided she wouldn't tell her dad.

She logged out of the computer and closed the edit room door behind her, wondering whether she should go home and shower or curl up under her desk and sleep until the morning shift started. She walked down the dim hallways of Atlas, passing by the studio door. The lights were off. The cameras had cloths draped over them. The great marble desk had been pushed to the corner. Without the crew, the lights, the hum of the morning bustle, the studio was just another gray room. It was missing its warm, attracting glow. But that had been gone for some time now.

She passed the green rooms, the hair and makeup chairs, the catering kitchen, and felt a pang of sadness. She'd miss coffee with Hallie and Wesley. The low lights and empty rooms made her feel lonely. Atlas *was* where she'd always wanted to be. She continued walking.

Had she not tried hard enough to make things better? Was she giving up too soon? The bravado from the morning had worn off. She didn't feel so strong in the dark.

The elevator dinged and she stepped inside, her heartbeat quickening. Had she acted irrationally? *Am I too young to make such a career-turning decision?* The questions swirled and she bit down hard on the inside of her cheek as the elevator walls seemed to close in.

What have I done?

Olivia raced back to the office, desperate to soothe her mind. It was too late to call her mom. Besides, she wouldn't really understand. Olivia knew she needed someone who had the experience of working in New York City. Who had heard all about Andrea and Ken. Who had studied Atlas and *Happy Hour* with her and listened to her stories about Violet's interviews and the celebrity guests. Who understood why she was panicking.

Olivia fumbled with the phone in her pocket. All the progress she'd made, all the sleep she'd caught up on and the healing she'd begun, would be destroyed if she kept working like this. She tried to remind herself of that as her fingers trembled.

She brought the phone to her ear and heard the dial tone, pacing up and down the row of desks. It was nearing 8:00 a.m. in London.

"Liv?" answered Gwen. "Why are you awake?"

Olivia's breath caught in her throat. She steadied herself against a desk. "You answered."

"I haven't heard from you in a while," said Gwen slowly. She didn't sound mad. If anything, her voice had a melancholy to it. "I've had to get all my information from Mom," Gwen said quietly.

Olivia touched the zipper on her sweater, feeling the cold metal against her fingers.

"Look, Gwen—" she started.

"No, Olivia, I should say—" interrupted Gwen.

"I'm sorry," they said in perfect unison.

She heard Gwen give a small laugh. She could picture her face, with her dimples and scrunched nose as she smiled. She imagined her sister's eyes crinkled at the corners and her strong brows raised in delight. She missed that face very much.

"Gwen," she felt her throat tighten before admitting, "I did something really bad today." She anxiously walked towards the back windows.

"What? Did you get back with Scott?" asked Gwen.

"No!" burst Olivia. "Never!" She peered out the window looking at the streetlights on Fifth Avenue. She was nervous Gwen was going to tell her she was an idiot. A fool for quitting. A selfish brat for only calling when it was convenient for her. If anything, she deserved the latter.

"But maybe this is worse." Olivia curled her free hand into a tiny fist against her skirt and held her breath. "I put my two weeks in at *Happy Hour.*"

She closed her eyes.

"Oh wow," breathed Gwen.

"Please don't yell at me," Olivia interjected. "I'm already regretting this so much. What am I going to do? I have nothing, I have no money!"

Olivia took a step back from the window. Maybe she could call Mary tomorrow and tell her it was a side effect of the medicine. That she'd experienced temporary amnesia. That she, of course, had made a mistake and there was nothing more in the world she wanted than to work at *Happy Hour*.

"Liv," soothed Gwen. "Liv, stop."

Olivia heaved short, shallow breaths into the receiver, gripping it tightly to her ear.

"I'm really proud of you."

Olivia's hand unclenched, she took a step back. A dumb smile spread across her face. "You are?"

"Yes!" exclaimed Gwen. "This show was killing you! And it was killing me watching you try so hard for the wrong job." Olivia nodded slowly as the words sunk in.

"There is so much to life outside of work," Gwen continued. Olivia noticed the strain in her voice, as if she'd been holding this in for far too long. "I know you're mad at me for moving to London, but it took me moving here to realize that. And I *need* you to know that it is true." Her voice was pleading.

Olivia turned back to the window, peering out at the Fifth Avenue lights once again. "So I didn't do the wrong thing?" squeaked Olivia.

"Not at all," assured Gwen. "Look, I'll help you find your next steps." Olivia felt her breathing begin to even. "Come to London first, take a break. De-stress. You'll love it here. You can see what I mean about there being more to life than work. I'm so happy you quit."

As she said those words Olivia felt the lump in her throat soften, the tightness in her chest ease. She cocked her head to the side. "Are you sure this is Gwen?" she asked through a small smile.

"Are you sure this is Olivia?"

~

As she packed up, Olivia noticed the glass door to Andrea's office was ajar. She took a few steps closer and peeked inside. Her eyes adjusted to the dark and she walked in farther.

It looked so different from her mother's office in North Carolina, which had been decorated with framed photos of her and Gwen and her dad, sticky notes from coworkers, flowers, pieces of art, trinkets from company parties. Andrea's office held nothing. The walls were bare, there were no photos of children, no semblance of a family. The desk had no notes or plants in bloom or colorful calendars. It lacked personality, humanity.

Olivia realized she didn't know Andrea at all.

And yet, Olivia could see herself becoming Andrea. She could see herself staying at *Happy Hour* and working her way up, coming in early and staying late. Continuing to ignore dinners and parties and dates. She'd push away her friends, her parents, her sister, anyone who got in the way of work. She could silence all hobbies, relationships, and cast them all so far out that she wouldn't mind working double shifts. If anything, she'd request them, just to fill her growing loneliness. If TV was really her dream, she would sacrifice everything.

Because one day, she could have her own office, too. And it would look exactly like Andrea's.

CHAPTER 19

The summer Olivia had learned how to swim, her mom was assigned to a business project that took her away to Charleston, South Carolina, for many weeks. This left her dad in charge of most things he'd only done a handful of times: picking Olivia up from soccer practice, taking her to friends' houses, doing her laundry.

Olivia didn't think much of it; she was only six. Instead of 6:30 p.m. dinner on the table like usual, her dad set up a picnic for him, Gwen, and Olivia on the living room floor. He laid out a beach towel and pillows for them to sit on and arranged their McDonald's Happy Meals on gingham placemats. The three of them ate together on the floor while WWE played on the TV. They watched bombastic wrestlers slam each other to the ground, flattening their opponents with metal chairs in between bites of fries, forever cementing the image of the The Undertaker—with his eyeliner and long stringy hair—in Olivia's mind every time she ordered fast food for years to come.

During the summer days, Olivia and Gwen would spend hours at their neighborhood pool. They loved being in the water and turned a shade of golden bronze that made them look even more like twins. The pool mothers gushed over their skin tones, teaching Olivia at a very young age the value in a good tan.

Gwen was on the swim team and could swim across the pool on her own, often joining friends in the deep end, playing mermaids and Marco Polo. Olivia, however, still needed the support of pink floaties around her arms and was confined to the shallower, less fun waters.

Gwen, being Gwen, had a plan for that.

"Swim to me, Livvy!" she would shout as Olivia doggie paddled to her, determined to have her sister join her everywhere she went. Even in their youth, Gwen had a way of leading Olivia toward success. By the end of the summer, the floaties had come off and Olivia was able to swim a few meters at a time before latching back on to the security of the pool's edge.

On a particularly breezy day in August, while their mom was still away in Charleston, their dad joined them in the deep end and led them over to the blue spiral slide. It glistened in the sun, the water squirting out from a small spigot at the top and softly cascading down into the pool.

"Are you ready to give it a try, Liv?" asked her dad. Olivia clung to his arms.

"Do it, Livvy!" squealed Gwen.

Olivia stared up at the slide, its ladder, its sharp twists and turns. It was located in the deepest corner of the pool. "You go first," responded Olivia tentatively.

Gwen climbed out of the pool and took several wet steps toward the base of the slide.

"Show us how it's done, Gwen!" called her father from the water.

Olivia watched her sister race up the ladder. "Okay, Livvy, you climb up like this," Gwen shouted. "And then you sit up here, see, with your feet down!" She perched at the top of the slide, her tiny ankles dangling over the incline. "Then don't look down because you'll get scared!" she called, her voice trailing higher at the end. Gwen grabbed the sides of the top rails and looked down below.

"Now let go!"

Olivia watched Gwen's body twist around the slide and into the water, making a tiny splash. Her head bobbed up with a great smile. "See!" She paddled over to her sister. "It's easy! Now you go!"

Olivia was still holding onto their dad. She looked up at his dark brown eyes.

"You can do it, kid." He nodded encouragingly. "I'll be here to catch you at the end."

"Promise?"

"Promise," replied her dad. "Plus you can swim, I've seen it!"

"Come on Olivia, it's fun!" cheered Gwen. She knew her sister wouldn't lie.

Her dad gave her a little push and she paddled to the side of the pool. Olivia pulled herself out of the water and slowly approached the ladder, knees shaking with every step. The ladder felt cold as she climbed up its steps and positioned herself on the slide's edge. The pool seemed so far down below. A shiver ran down her spine.

"Don't look down, Liv! Just let go!" she heard Gwen call from the water. She seemed miles away.

If Gwen can do it, then so can I, she reassured herself. Olivia released her hands from the railings and let the momentum of the water stream carry her down. She felt her legs twist and her body turn, and within seconds, she shot out into the deep end. Immediately, her father's warm arms wrapped around her. She coughed and sputtered, wiping the chlorine from her eyes. A feeling of accomplishment overcame her. She did it. And it was … amazing!

She looked up and watched a grin fill her father's face. "Good job, Liv!"

"Yay Livvy! Let's go again!" Gwen was already out of the water and back up the slide.

The sisters took turns going down the slide over and over again. Each time, Olivia's dad caught her in his arms and she clung on to him tightly until it was her turn to climb up the ladder again. By the time she mastered the slide, the sun had begun to set and the pool crowd had thinned out.

"Alright girls," announced their father. "Time to go."

"Noooo. Please Dad!" begged Olivia. "One more time?"

Their father carried her over to the edge of the pool. "No, you've had enough on the slide. Let's get out and get dressed." He lifted Olivia out of the water.

Gwen stuck out her bottom lip. "I want to go one more time, too!"

Olivia had learned at a young age that there were two types of parents in the world. Ones who let their kids eat donuts for breakfast and scream in the middle of Target, and others who, like her father, didn't repeat themselves.

Their father gave Olivia and Gwen a look so stern they instantly closed their mouths. Gwen climbed out of the water and stood beside Olivia shivering.

"Girls, I'm going to the men's room to change." He handed them their towels. "You stay put here with our bags. I'll just be a minute."

They watched their father walk along the pool deck and behind the wooden panels of the men's changing room. Gwen's hair was dripping onto Olivia's shoulder. She watched it trickle down her arm, like the water stream at the top of the slide.

"Gwen," whispered Olivia, a devilish smile creeping onto her face. "What if we go down one more time?"

She watched her sister shake her head. "Dad said to wait here."

"He won't know!" pleaded Olivia. This was like the first time she'd tried red velvet cake. She loved it so much she couldn't picture another day without it. "You wanted to go again! Just one more time." She pushed her sister toward the slide. "You first!"

Gwen hesitated, a look of concern on her face.

"Come on!" Olivia gave her a nudge again. "You said! It will be quick."

Gwen's expression softened as she looked around the pool for signs of their dad. "Okay, okay, fine! Really quick," agreed Gwen, her smile revealing her newest missing tooth. Olivia clapped excitedly.

Gwen sped to the ladder and expertly climbed to the top. She wasted no time flinging herself down the slide, hands in the air as she splashed into the water. She bobbed back up.

"Your turn, Liv!" she called from the water. "Go quick!"

Olivia grabbed a kickboard from the pool's edge. "Keep that at the bottom so I can use it to float!" she declared, throwing it into the water. She was proud of herself for engineering such a plan.

Her feet started climbing the ladder before she had time to think. Her dad would be out in seconds. If he caught her, she'd be cooked.

Olivia looked out from the top of the slide. The pool seemed even bigger without her father at the bottom. The kickboard looked much smaller than his strong arms. She gulped.

Gwen gestured for Olivia to slide down. It was too late to change her mind now. She let her hands go from the rails.

Olivia heard the whoosh of the air, the splash of water as she broke the pool's surface. Her head was under within seconds. She reached out for the kickboard, flailing her arms as she tried to grab ahold, but couldn't find it. Her head dipped under the water as she kicked and waved, still searching for the board. She began to sink deeper and deeper underwater. Her legs and arms thrashed wildly, the light above the surface fading as her lungs called for air. Without her dad's arms, she couldn't find her way out. Her desperate hands reached for something, anything.

Just as the light above was about to fade completely, she gave one last kick with all her might.

Her arms collided with the kickboard overhead. She grabbed its edges tightly, and with another kick, her head broke through the water. Air filled her lungs. She gasped and turned to see her sister swimming frantically toward her. Gwen had been too far away to help.

Olivia turned back toward the pool's edge, and with the gentle guidance of her sister, she climbed out of the water. She clutched her towel over her shaking body and began to cry.

"Don't cry, Liv! It's okay. Dad didn't catch us!" Gwen consoled her sister. "Besides, you swam! You did it on your own!"

"I know, but I was so scared."

SPRING

CHAPTER 20

It was the end of March. The gray in the city had given way to the subtle undertones of spring. It was still chilly, but the sting to the winter air had faded, the birds had returned, and green grass appeared in the small parks and along square patches on the sidewalks.

Olivia looked out the window of the double decker plane as it turned onto the runway. It was nighttime now. The moon was clear and bright against the sky. She anxiously wiggled her toes.

Just a few weeks ago, Olivia had walked home from Atlas for the last time.

She'd met Wesley and Hallie immediately in the cafeteria after her last show and thrown her arms around them both. "If I didn't have you two here, I wouldn't have made it this long," she confessed. She looked at Hallie. "You really saved me. Metaphorically and you know," she clutched her stomach and mimed throwing up, "—literally." Hallie laughed as she hugged her back.

"Any plans for what's next?" Wesley had asked.

Olivia had bitten her lip as she thought about this. "I have some ideas," she mused.

It was true, she had been thinking about her next move. In fact, she spent most of her nights on her old MacBook from college, partially because she couldn't bear to look at a TV screen, but also because there were so many thoughts in her head that she needed to get out. Just typing them in a Word document made her feel better. But she wasn't ready to talk about anything just yet. She was too tired, too burnt out. There was something important she needed to do first.

"I'm actually going to London," Olivia answered. "All my unused vacation days were enough to pay for my ticket."

"That's tragic, but inspiring," stated Hallie. Wesley nodded in agreement.

Olivia left that day after looking up at the gods in the Atlas lobby one last time. Their facial expressions looked less serene and more morose than ever. She gave a small wave, knowing she didn't need their looking after anymore.

Walking along the white marble floors, a powerful royal blue pantsuit and a dark bob caught her eye. Olivia stood taller, smoothed her hair, and called, "Violet!" She quickly walked a few steps toward the anchor.

Violet turned around as Olivia stuck out her hand. "I'm Olivia, we've only met a few times," she said calmly. Violet matched her firm handshake. "I wanted to say thanks for the opportunity." She looked out across the great lobby. "Today is my last day at *Happy Hour*."

Violet's brown eyes looked into hers. Olivia watched Violet's sharp features soften the way they did whenever she ended a heartfelt segment.

"I know who you are," Violet said quietly. "I'm sorry to see you go."

Olivia's cheeks flushed. She tucked her hair behind her ear. Violet Jones knew who *she* was?

"Me too," Olivia offered. Violet held her gaze as she stood unmoving in her blue pantsuit. "Well, thanks again," said

Olivia, smiling and turning toward the revolving doors. She didn't expect anything else from Violet; the fact she knew of her existence was enough.

"My notecards from you were always perfect."

Olivia looked over her shoulder as Violet spoke her parting words. A feeling of immense pride swelled in her chest.

Olivia beamed and thanked Violet again. Only now Olivia wasn't as quick to walk away. She had a feeling, a sneaking suspicion, there was more Violet wanted to say. Did she silently agree with Olivia's choice to leave and follow another path? If she knew of Olivia, did she also know what life was like behind the camera?

Or would she urge Olivia to stay, encouraging her that if she just pushed a little more, she could be like her. That it all *would* work out. Olivia held her breath as Violet opened her mouth to speak.

"Well, I'm sure hundreds of eager candidates will be after your role. Good luck."

Violet smiled and took off across the lobby, leaving Olivia frozen to the floor. She knew Violet wasn't wrong.

Olivia came home that day to a cupcake from Jess. Olivia hugged her and insisted they cut it down the middle. They sat on their couch later that night, Jess painting her nails and Olivia typing away on her laptop.

"Margot hasn't been around lately," Jess had pointed out, shaking a bottle of light pink polish.

Olivia had told Margot she'd quit *Happy Hour*, and suggested they meet up soon, maybe walk around Central Park or grab coffee like old times. Margot said she'd check with Ben to find a free weekend.

"Margot's still on Boyfriend Island," Olivia said around a frown. She looked up from her laptop. "I don't know what more I can do besides be patient. I know I was kind of unreachable, too," she confessed.

"I've had that happen before," lamented Jess. She carefully painted her pointer finger. "I like to think that good friends find their way back." Olivia had really grown to like her.

"I hope so," Olivia voiced.

~

The engine of the plane roared to life as Olivia replayed her conversation with Jess. She missed Margot and hoped she would see her soon after her trip. But for now, her focus was on another resident of Boyfriend Island, Gwen.

The flooring rumbled beneath her feet as the plane jetted down the runway and lifted its wheels, climbing higher and higher away from New York, putting distance between Olivia and the city. She loved her home, but she was eager to claim some space. Too much had happened without pause, and she needed a rest. She wanted to clear her mind, reassess her priorities, and be with the one person who always helped her find herself, even if she *was* still a little let down.

She soared higher into the darkness, the twinkling lights from the city fading until they were replaced by the ocean. It would be 8:00 a.m. sharp when she arrived in London. With every mile she was leaving behind the night and inching closer to a new day, a new light.

What will London be like? she thought as she snuggled under the thin blanket given to her by the flight attendant. Had Gwen already adopted UK fashion and makeup trends, switching to the heavy foundation and thick eyebrow look Olivia had seen on social media? What if she had an accent like Madonna? Olivia smiled to herself. No, that wasn't like Gwen. The bigger question was: What would Henry be like?

Olivia must've dozed off over the Atlantic. Her next memory was a gentle tap on her shoulder from the flight attendant.

"Miss? I'm pleased to tell you we've landed in London."

CHAPTER 21

"You're here!" Gwen squealed as she pulled Olivia into a tight embrace just outside the arrivals gate. The bouquet of flowers in her hand brushed against the back of Olivia's neck. The hug felt just as warm and comforting as always. Olivia wasn't sure why she was expecting it to feel different. She breathed a sigh of relief, glad she had a week of Gwen's attention and affection ahead. Everything would be okay now; they were together. Her shoulders relaxed as she beamed at her sister.

Gwen looked the same, but somehow brighter. Her hazel eyes were clear and golden, her hair was shiny and shorter, sitting just on top of her narrow collarbone. She wore a vivid pink sweater that lit up her whole face. *Gwen never wore such a color in New York—*

"Welcome to London!" An English male voice interrupted her thoughts.

Olivia tore her eyes away from the glowing Gwen to look up at Henry. He'd been standing beside Gwen all along, a matching smile wide across his face. She didn't realize he'd be so … tall. Henry stood at least a foot over Gwen, with smooth dark brown hair, a narrow face, and light brown eyes.

"We're so happy to have you!" he continued. Olivia hugged him the same stiff way she hugged her distant Uncle Roy.

"It's nice to meet you," she stated formally.

Henry smiled again, his eyes soft, friendly. "Likewise. I've heard so much about you."

Olivia felt guilty she couldn't say the same.

Gwen handed her the bouquet of flowers while Henry politely grabbed her suitcase and backpack. Olivia was taken aback by the kind gesture. She could count on one hand the number of times anyone in New York had offered their help. Yet she found herself annoyed. Did Henry not think she was capable of carrying her own things?

Her sister grinned as she linked arms with Olivia and led them out of the airport. Olivia exhaled slowly and tried to savor the moment. She'd been waiting for this chance to be reunited with Gwen. *Just the two of us.* She hummed to herself at the thought. "My car's just over here!" Henry's happy voice punctured the air. *And Henry.*

Thirty minutes into their drive, Olivia's brain dizzy from trying to reason why they were driving on the wrong side of the road, they crossed a small bridge. "Olivia, look to your left!" announced Henry, letting go of Gwen's hand to point out the window.

Olivia turned and saw Big Ben in the distance. Like Henry, it too, was taller than she expected. She stared at the clock tower and then looked across the river to glimpse the London Eye. It glimmered in the morning sunlight. Olivia thought London wasn't supposed to be sunny.

"Beautiful day, isn't it?" remarked Henry, reaching for Gwen's hand again.

They turned down a street lined with white brick row houses. Olivia instantly noticed the bright pink and blue doors that Gwen had told her about when she'd first moved. It reminded her of scenes from *The Parent Trap* or *Love Actually*, the way the homes were connected so tightly together, sharing small courtyards in the front. Magnolia trees dotted the sidewalks, their pink petals just nearly in bloom.

Henry parked in front of a row house with a light blue door and shut off the engine.

"Home!" Gwen announced. She stepped out of the car and unlocked their small front gate. A wave of tiredness ran through Olivia's body. After all, it was still the middle of the night in New York. She had a vision of Hallie getting ready for work.

Henry followed behind with Olivia's bags again. "Let's unpack your stuff in my room," said Gwen, pushing open the light blue door. She led them up several flights of stairs, past the living room and the kitchen, to a small spare bedroom with a slanted roof and a skylight window just above the bed. Olivia noticed Gwen's flat had many different floors with varying amounts of steps in between each. The kitchen was on one floor, the bathroom on another, and the bedrooms up top.

"I'll let you two catch up while I start the roast." Henry delicately placed Olivia's backpack on the bed. "Make yourself at home, Olivia," he said, smiling again. *Why is he so smiley? And what is a roast?*

Olivia sat on the duvet and took in the bedroom.

Instead of the framed prints of Italy on the walls, Gwen's room had abstract watercolors and Picasso prints. Gone were the parquet floors of New York City, replaced by a cream-colored carpet with a blue oriental rug on top. A snake plant sat in the corner in a large terracotta pot. Olivia's mind reached back to the not one but two separate philodendrons she and Gwen had bought at the Union Square Farmers Market and promptly mis-watered and killed within weeks.

"You're so quiet," said Gwen, placing one of Olivia's shirts in the bottom drawer of a tall brown dresser. "Is everything okay?"

Olivia gave a halfhearted nod. The essence of Gwen that she knew in New York was undetectable. Their apartment together had felt so comfortable, so safe. She now felt like she was in a stranger's home.

"I'm just tired," answered Olivia, zipping her empty suitcase shut and placing it in the corner. "And I have to pee." She stood and went down the flight of stairs to the bathroom. The handle stuck when she tried to open the door.

"Just a moment!" called Henry from inside.

"Oh, uh, sorry!" Olivia answered, racing back up the steps.

She returned to the room and let out a yawn, feeling embarrassed to admit to Gwen that she didn't realize Henry would be around so much.

"Want to take a nap?" Gwen asked, closing the curtains. "It'll help with the jet lag."

What Olivia really wanted was alone time with Gwen. So they could talk and catch up—more than just a few minutes of unpacking. There were still thoughts on her mind that only Gwen could understand, ideas she desperately wanted to share with her.

Gwen walked toward the bed and pulled back the sheets. "Here, I'll wake you in a few hours."

She turned and shut off the lights. "Henry's making a roast!" she exclaimed, "You'll love it." She smiled and pulled the door shut behind her. Olivia heard her skip down the stairs, calling Henry's name.

Olivia slowly climbed into the bed. She still had to pee. And she still didn't know what a "roast" meant. She stared up into the skylight, watching the thin clouds pass by until she fell asleep.

~

A few hours later, Olivia stirred and heard the sound of Gwen's laugh, the tinkering of utensils against ceramic plates, the opening and shutting of the kitchen cabinets. Rolling to her side, she checked the time on her phone. It was late afternoon. The show would've finished just a few hours ago. Olivia wondered how long it would take before she stopped comparing time to *Happy Hour*. Her stomach rumbled and she decided to go downstairs.

The kitchen table was set with big white plates and cloth napkins. The flowers from Gwen stood as the centerpiece in a clear vase. Two small candles sat on the window ledge just above the table. Olivia could see the pink magnolia tree glistening in the golden hour.

Gwen was laying out the last set of silverware when she saw Olivia pad down the steps.

"You're up!" she mused. "Do you want a drink? Henry makes a mean gin and tonic."

Henry turned around from behind the stove. He waved to her with a pair of tongs. A tray of roasted vegetables lay on the black granite counter beside him. Gwen stood and opened a cabinet, pulling out a glass bottle of gin. "We got this on holiday a few weeks ago!" she exclaimed. "It's our favorite."

Olivia raised an eyebrow. *Holiday?*

She watched Gwen pull three cocktail glasses from the cupboard and retrieve a lime from the fruit basket. She then took out metal utensils that Olivia could only classify as "cocktail tools." She didn't know much about mixology and didn't think Gwen did either. "It was a bank holiday, so we just popped up to Scotland," she continued, turning to Henry and smiling. "It was really lovely. You'd like it, Liv."

"Cool," Olivia responded. She helped herself to a glass of water.

Henry pulled a large piece of beef from the oven. "Looks great," announced Gwen. She walked over and affectionately rubbed Henry's shoulders. Olivia turned away.

While she'd hoped they'd go out to dinner, maybe get sushi like old times, the dinner did look really nice. It smelled good too. If she was being honest with herself, Olivia didn't see anything particularly wrong with Henry. He was just … in the way. Olivia was reminded she had to use the bathroom.

She started toward the flight of stairs just as Henry moved away from the oven. They both stopped at the bottom step and turned to each other.

"Er, bathroom," Olivia explained.

"Ah, that's where I was headed too. Ladies first!" Henry said politely. He gestured for Olivia to go ahead. She had a feeling it was going to be a long week.

By nightfall, she was exhausted.

"Ready for bed?" asked Gwen as Olivia stifled a yawn at the table.

Olivia nodded and they cleared the kitchen together, scraping the little that remained on their plates into the trash. Henry moved to the living room couch, opening a book, as Olivia and Gwen climbed the stairs.

"So? What do you think?" Gwen asked nervously, shutting the bedroom door behind her.

Olivia picked up her brush and walked over to the small mirror beside the window. "London's nice," she answered. She ran the bristles through her hair.

"I mean about Henry!" Gwen whispered, sitting down on the corner of the bed. She looked up at her sister expectantly.

Olivia remained facing the mirror. "He's nice, too," she said quickly.

She watched Gwen's face fall in the reflection. "That's all?" she whimpered.

Olivia turned and placed her brush on the dresser. "Look, Gwen," she sat beside her sister on the bed, trying to choose her words carefully. She wasn't sure how this different, new Gwen would react.

"Henry is fine. He's great." Olivia waved her hand dismissively. "I just thought *we* would have some time together. The two of us."

Gwen's crestfallen look made Olivia feel worse. She'd chosen to tell Gwen the truth and it'd still upset her. Their honesty was always something they could fall back on. It was a core element of their relationship, even when they disagreed. *Had that changed too?*

"But you can say anything you want in front of Henry!" Gwen said reassuringly. "I promise, he gets it. He's *one of us.*" Gwen urged.

Olivia eyed her skeptically. She'd thought Margot had fit that description once too.

Gwen looked her sister in the eye. "Instead of having one person to talk to, now you have two. Don't you believe me?"

Olivia stood up and walked to the other side of the bed, peeling back the covers. "I honestly don't know what to believe anymore," sighed Olivia. "I just want to spend time with you."

It was the first time all day Gwen's eyes didn't seem as bright.

"Of course we'll do things just me and you," she explained quietly. She pushed herself to her feet and walked toward the door. "I just really wanted you to like him."

Olivia crawled into bed while Gwen shut off the lights. She wanted to believe Gwen. She hoped Henry could become someone she trusted. But something about him didn't fit into the equation of two sisters. It had always been just the two of them. Now Gwen was here in London with a new life and Olivia couldn't relate. It didn't matter how nice he was, Olivia wanted Gwen's attention and Henry, whether he meant to or not, had it more.

Her stomach had a sinking feeling—not like the ulcer, but in a way that matched her intuition. She knew the real truth. Henry wasn't out of place. She was.

CHAPTER 22

Sunlight streamed across the white duvet from the skylight overhead. Olivia could hear Gwen and Henry downstairs, their laughs traveling through the thin walls. With a long yawn, Olivia reached for her phone and dialed her mom; with the five-hour time difference it was just after 7:30 a.m. in North Carolina. Gwen had let her sleep in late.

Olivia sat cross-legged on the bed while she described London to her mother, mentioning the blue and pink doors, the narrow streets, the varying heights of Big Ben and Henry.

"And how *is* Henry?" her mom asked carefully. Olivia heard the rustle of the newspaper and imagined her mom doing the morning crossword puzzle.

"He's fine," she answered, lowering her voice. She moved off the bed and walked toward the back window, away from the door. "I mean, he and Gwen do things like cook dinner and drink gin now." She rolled her eyes. "She never wanted to do those things with me."

Olivia chewed her lip as she looked out the window. It was another bright day in London. The shrubs in the back-yard swayed in the breeze. She spotted an orange cat walking along the neighbor's patio.

"She's adapting to a new way of life," her mom offered gently. "This has been a big change for her. Maybe cut her a little bit of slack?"

The cat jumped up onto the side fence that separated the two yards. Olivia was surprised such a large cat could stand on the narrow fence. It walked it like a tightrope toward the back brick wall. "She just seems so different," sighed Olivia. "I wanted to see the same old Gwen."

"Have you ever thought that maybe you seem different to her, too?" her mom asked. The cat reached the back wall and gingerly touched its nose to the brick. The wall was significantly higher than the fence. Olivia waited for the cat to turn around, realizing the pathway was blocked.

Olivia thought back to the last time she saw Gwen in person. She had still been excited about her promotion, still hopeful *Happy Hour* could bring her joy. Still in good health and not eager to put space between her and the city.

The cat moved its head up and down, as if it was surveying the jump, taking measurements. Its orange tail lay flat. Olivia realized she was holding her breath as she watched.

In one great motion that cat shot upward, all four paws landing delicately on top of the brick wall. It quickly scurried out of sight.

"Yeah, alright," grumbled Olivia. "I get your point."

~

That afternoon, Gwen had told Olivia to prepare for afternoon tea. "It's a beautiful and refined tradition," Gwen gushed. "The one I picked for us is extra special."

Us? She and Gwen were *finally* going to have their sister time! A smile stretched across Olivia's face. "That sounds really great!" She gave Gwen a hug.

Olivia made a mental checklist of all the things she wanted to discuss at tea while she got dressed. She borrowed a houndstooth skirt from Gwen and pulled on tights and black boots. She matched it with a white button-down blouse, feeling like she'd accomplished the look of a British schoolgirl. She lent Gwen an olive green sweater. It felt nice to share clothes again.

Gwen stood by the bathroom door as Olivia curled her hair in big, loose waves.

"Want me to do it?" she offered.

It was just like old times, Gwen gently sectioning off her hair and soothingly brushing each piece before wrapping it around the iron.

They walked downstairs, smelling of perfume and hairspray. Olivia felt giddy.

Then he saw Henry emerge into the kitchen, dressed in a white button-down and slacks. "Ready?" he asked. "I love afternoon tea."

Olivia shut her eyes before anything could happen. The world hadn't ended on her in months. She desperately wanted to keep it that way.

Instead, she filled a glass with water and sipped it slowly, moving to sit at the kitchen table. She shot Gwen a low, glaring look.

"Trust me," Gwen mouthed.

"No!" Olivia mouthed back.

Gwen laughed and walked toward her sister, pulling her into a tight embrace. Olivia stayed stiff. Gwen hugged tighter. Olivia could feel Gwen still shaking with laughter, knowing her sister loved and hated this hug at the same time. It made Olivia start laughing too.

The three of them took the Tube to Covent Garden just on the other side of the Thames. Olivia didn't see any rats or stray pieces of pizza. There wasn't even a loose newspaper or tissue. The London public train system was shockingly clean. She laughed to herself, realizing that was probably the first time her brain ever put the words "train" and "clean" together in a sentence.

She did, however, see a woman struggling to maneuver a pink vinyl sofa onto three open seats. She snuck a picture and sent it to Margot.

"I think I won the game."

Olivia texted.

"LOL I think u did."

Margot responded immediately.

Olivia didn't know what to think of their friendship anymore. Maybe they would find their way back.

It was just past four o'clock when they arrived at The Savoy. The host led them to a large dining room with a great glass dome. It filled the room with sunlight, highlighting the ornate crown molding and golden wall sconces. A stunning grand piano decorated the center, where a man in a tuxedo delicately danced his fingers across the keys. Olivia didn't frequent many nice restaurants in New York, but she had a feeling they didn't look like this. Gwen nudged her as she caught Olivia staring at the pianist. "See what I mean?" she whispered.

A waiter placed a white cloth napkin over Olivia's lap. Another laid out silverware next to the cerulean blue and white china. Their crystal flute glasses were filled with bubbling champagne.

"This is really nice," confessed Olivia. She couldn't remember the last time she'd experienced fine dining. Actually, had she *ever* experienced fine dining?

Gwen and Henry smiled at each other. "Just wait until you see the sandwiches." Gwen winked.

"And the cakes!" chimed Henry.

As if they were cued by a director, three waiters brought out five-tiered silver stands with finger sandwiches and tiny pastries. The sweets were colorful and petite, with intricate icing designs and flowers made of sugar. They looked too beautiful to eat. Large scones filled the middle tiers, with jam and what looked like a large cup of marshmallow fluff.

"That's clotted cream," explained Gwen. "It's even better than butter."

Olivia nodded and took in their sight of all the different foods. "No need to rush," Henry commented, as if he were reading Olivia's mind. "Afternoon tea is all about relaxing and enjoying."

She smiled and eyed a cucumber sandwich. "I haven't relaxed in years," she admitted.

"Yeah, twenty-five to be exact," joked Gwen.

They took their time sampling the different sandwiches, cutting into the tiny passion fruit and lemon cakes and sipping their tea. Olivia watched in horror as Gwen poured milk into her teacup. Henry laughed. "Try it!" he urged. Olivia tentatively added a few drips into her Earl Grey. It was actually pretty good.

Their champagne glasses magically refilled every half hour; their conversation flowed as they relaxed more and more. Olivia learned that Henry was also the youngest in his family, having one older brother and one older sister. He'd spent much of his youth at boarding school, which was common for boys in London. It was there he discovered his natural ability for tennis.

"Henry almost went pro!" boasted Gwen, patting his arm.

Olivia saw him blush. "Really?" She figured his wingspan alone could cover half the court.

"Yes," he admitted. "I trained three times a day. It got to the point where I stopped seeing my friends and started taking classes that didn't interest me just because they gave less homework." He picked up a curried chicken salad sandwich. "It became my whole life." He took a bite and chewed thoughtfully.

A waiter came by and refilled their champagne glasses again.

"Why did you stop?" Olivia asked gently.

Henry looked up at her with melancholic eyes. "I was dedicating so much to tennis, and I wasn't even certain I'd make pro." He pushed the crumbs around on his plate. "I wasn't even certain going pro would make me happy."

Olivia studied his face. It was as if she could see him reliving his decision. "Anyway," said Henry, reaching for his champagne, "by the end of it, I resented tennis for taking away so many of my school experiences."

Olivia and Gwen exchanged a sad look. Henry wasn't much older than Luke or Drew, but Olivia couldn't imagine having a conversation like this with either of them. It was refreshing the way Henry could speak so openly about his hurt and disappointment, his feelings of letdown and regret.

"But it all worked out," said Gwen, grabbing Henry's hand. "You love practicing law. I can see the joy it brings you."

He affectionately squeezed Gwen's hand and smiled at her. "Now," he continued, "I win *in* the court instead of on it."

Olivia laughed and Gwen rolled her eyes. She heard Gwen's voice in her head echoing, *Instead of having one person to talk to, now you have two.*

Olivia placed her napkin on the table and stood up, noticing Henry was on his feet as well. "Let me guess, bathroom?" They laughed again.

Henry wasn't going to win her over in one tea, but Olivia could see why Gwen liked him.

He was honest. Devoid of ego and the terrible show-off quality possessed by so many men in New York City. Olivia saw it in the way he carried himself, in the way he asked her questions and took real interest in her answers. She saw it in the way he looked at Gwen or patted her hand. He was genuine.

"I know you're still finding your next move," said Henry after they both had returned to the table. The waiters hustled around them, clearing their used plates, refilling their teapots. "But I really think you'll be happy once you do."

Olivia leaned back in her chair. Full from the sandwiches, the cakes, the clotted cream. Whether it was the peaceful piano music or the refills of champagne, she felt calmer.

She looked between Gwen and Henry, both faces staring intently back at hers. She smiled. "I hope so."

CHAPTER 23

The sun stayed for another day but was replaced by patches of fog and light rain throughout the week. It was bound to happen; it *was* London after all.

But Olivia didn't mind. Gwen had taken off work, leaving the sisters alone to fill their days with sightseeing and exploring the city.

Gwen showed her the shops on Oxford Street, the narrow alleyways in Soho, the colorful string lights and red lanterns in Chinatown. They grabbed fish and chips in Borough Market, walked the Millennium Bridge, and watched the swans in St. James Park. Olivia nearly tripped when she spotted Huxley Major on the streets of Chelsea in a bright red fedora. He starred in the trashy, yet wildly popular reality show that they watched with Henry at night called *Brixton Babes*. It made her think of Hallie and Wesley and their gift from Brad Bradley.

The feeling of comfort around Gwen slowly returned. The effort of conversation was less strained without Henry, even though Olivia had started to get used to his presence. They talked about Gwen's job, her new friends, what it was like to have free health care. Most importantly, Olivia discovered she and Gwen's sister language was not lost. One night, over steak and ale pies with Henry, the sisters guided him through an act-by-act analysis of *Weekend at Beanies*, tears of laughter streaming down their faces.

At the end of the week, Gwen and Olivia decided to visit a coffee shop on the high street in Battersea. It was just a short walk-through Clapham Common from their flat. The sky was cloudy, but the sun peeked out in between the thick cumulus shapes. Olivia could smell spring in the air as they walked through the park, the freshly cut grass, the flowers in bloom, the earthy soil. She sneezed.

"Are you feeling better?" Gwen asked as they brought their drinks to a table near the window and sat down. "More refreshed, less stressed?"

Olivia poured milk into her English Breakfast tea. "Yes," she nodded, giving the liquid a stir. "I feel a lot less overwhelmed. I thought I'd lost you," she admitted. "But I'm glad I didn't."

Gwen smiled and cut their piece of raspberry loaf in half. It was nice to see her eating sweets regularly. Olivia thought she'd been so rigid with her diet and exercise routine in New York.

She didn't know if she'd ever fully accept that Gwen lived in London. That her sister wouldn't always be awake to answer her calls or around to hug her despite her protests. She looked out the window, watching the passersby on the high street: a woman with her child, a man with a briefcase, a strong guy in a rugby uniform, his muscles visible through his shirt. Olivia suddenly wished rugby was a more popular sport in the US.

"Do you have an idea of what you want to do next?" Gwen asked, breaking off another small piece of the cake and popping it into her mouth. Olivia turned back to her sister.

"Sort of." She hummed, knowing Gwen wasn't talking about their next tourist activity. She speared a square of cake onto her fork and let the sweetness of the raspberry fill her mouth.

"Well, do you want to talk about it?" Olivia could see Gwen putting on her metaphorical big-sister hat.

Olivia grinned. "I'm actually okay."

There was no sarcasm in her voice. It was true, she *was* okay. She knew when she got back to the city, she'd contact a temp agency so she could work and pay her rent while she looked for a new job. She had given up Atlas but wasn't ready to leave television. Her time in the industry taught her about other networks and production companies with roles in marketing or development, helping promote the shows or even create them. Olivia could see herself enjoying something like that. She explained this to Gwen.

Gwen's eyebrows raised. "Wow, that's great!"

Without Gwen's constant availability, Olivia had been forced to think about her next move on her own. Researching companies online, texting Wesley and Hallie, even emailing alumni from her school. Everyone had helped guide her toward potential next roles, but Jess had put another idea in Olivia's mind.

The night Jess had given her the celebratory cupcake in their apartment, they had sat on the couch together. Just as Jess had finished painting her nails, she looked over at Olivia typing away on her MacBook and asked, "Why are you smiling?"

Olivia looked up from her laptop. "I didn't realize I was! I'm just writing a little story."

Jess laughed, "Well it looks like it makes you really happy."

The idea to write had already been on Olivia's mind, but Jess highlighted how good it made her feel. Olivia loved creating stories, imaging scenarios that didn't exist, taking note in her internal dialogue about the little details she was constantly observing. She wondered if she could turn it into something more.

Olivia smiled and pushed the last bite of cake toward Gwen. A gap in the clouds allowed the sun to stream brightly through the window. "I know it's a far-fetched dream and all," she hesitated, "but I'm also working on a pilot script."

She looked into Gwen's eyes and braced herself, waiting for Gwen to agree that it *was* a far-fetched dream.

"A pilot is the first episode of a TV series, by the way," she added quickly. "It's what writers submit to networks or writing competitions to get noticed."

"Ah, got it," said Gwen, still nodding and contemplating her response.

Olivia sat back in the chair. She knew most TV pilot scripts never made it out from the bottom of a box in some agent's office. That for every good idea she had, some other writer had three more. The percentage of no-name writers ever standing a chance to get noticed was very low.

The sunlight illuminated the gold flecks of Gwen's irises. "If anyone can do it, it's you." She beamed. "Do I get to read it?"

Olivia laughed and nodded.

They sat in the window a while longer, until the sun dipped just below the trees at the edge of the park. The tiny bit of tea left in the bottom of Olivia's cup had turned cold; only crumbs remained on their shared plate. Olivia looked out into the orange glow left in the sky. She didn't know exactly what would follow her return to New York City the next day, but she didn't feel afraid.

The little coffee shop had cleared out, leaving them with the low hum of the espresso machine, the softened lights as the barista began closing for the day.

Olivia didn't want to admit it, but London was nicer than she expected. The city that stole her sister was surprisingly peaceful.

CHAPTER 24

When Olivia pushed open the door to her New York City apartment, her first thought was that the inside looked smaller. It smelled different too. Musty. She wheeled her suitcase down the hall. The wooden floors looked dull, her couch gray and worn. The white kitchen counters were marked with various nicks and food stains. *Has it always been this way?*

She turned on the lamp in the living room. Jess wasn't home. Olivia figured she was probably out to dinner. She dropped her backpack in her room and yawned while walking to the shower.

As she lathered her hair with shampoo, she became aware she was alone again. The safety of Gwen gone, the excitement of travel now behind her. It was time to start something new.

Olivia had meant to create a list of to-do items during the flight home to better organize her next steps, but a fit of writing inspiration struck her just as the plane met the sky. By the time she touched down in JFK, she'd finished the ending to her pilot script. It was a neat fifty pages. She eagerly sent it to Gwen.

She turned off the shower and returned to her room, then sat on her bed in her towel. She typed out a text to Margot:

"Back from London. You around this week?"

She stared at it for a moment before deleting the words and putting her phone down. She changed into her pajamas instead and made a cup of tea, stealing some of Jess's milk and borrowing her "Twin Cities" mug (she couldn't bear to use a *Happy Hour* one). She curled into her bed and streamed two old episodes of *Brixton Babes* on her laptop, laughing at their funny accents before falling asleep.

~

Olivia awoke early the next morning and saw her clock read 3:00 a.m. A brief moment of panic ran through her body. It had been weeks since she'd last seen the clock on her dresser show that time.

She felt relief knowing it was the jet lag waking her so early. While she was grateful she didn't have to go into the office, she missed that she had something counting on her, expecting her. Something worth waking up for. It was going to take some getting used to, her not having a place to be.

Olivia quietly pulled her laptop from her backpack and sat in her bed until the sun rose, applying for jobs and even submitting her pilot script to a few programs she'd bookmarked. Many networks were now accepting summer applications for fellowships to join their writers' rooms. She knew it was ambitious, but she applied anyway.

After that, she unpacked her suitcase and freshened up her room, wiping the window and dusting the nightstand. She moved to the living room and pulled back the curtains to let the morning sunlight stream in. She rearranged the couch pillows and cleaned the coffee table, moving slowly so she wouldn't wake Jess. When the sun had risen enough to fully illuminate the room, Olivia took it as a cue to go outside and greet it.

She pulled on a light sweatshirt and sneakers and walked down the steps of her apartment building, noticing the tiny trees on her street boasted new green leaves. The trees weren't as big or colorful as Gwen's magnolias, but they looked nice. The sweet aromas from the bagel shop on the corner filled her nose. She'd always wanted to stop by, but the line was so long on the weekends. This Monday morning, the line was considerably shorter. She joined at the end, relishing that she had nowhere she needed to rush off to or go next. Once she started temping, that would change, of course, but for now, she enjoyed letting the morning pass as she stood and waited.

Olivia collected her brown bag with her poppyseed bagel and walked across the street to the small park along Second Avenue. The traffic in the East Village was quieter than the noisy streets around Atlas. She could hear the birds singing. Olivia sat on a metal bench and rolled up her sleeves, letting the sunlight kiss her skin. As she unwrapped her bagel, finding the cream cheese to bagel ratio quite pleasing, she had a realization. She liked New York City in the morning.

CHAPTER 25

Spring lasts roughly four weeks in the city before the sweltering heat and humidity of summer set in. The streets fill with tourists; the parks are dotted with picnics and frisbees and running dogs. Mister Softee trucks appear on seemingly every block; kids and adults alike clamoring to get their hands on a vanilla cone with rainbow sprinkles. The subways become saunas, the bodegas welcomed cool respites, and the air conditioning units in apartment windows begin to drip questionable fluids onto unlucky passersby below.

Olivia watched a splat of murky condensation fall directly onto a bald man's head as she walked behind him down Third Avenue. She quickly skirted by, careful not to scrape her new strappy sandals that showed off her fresh pedicure against the concrete. A matching red color adorned the nails on her hands. She didn't mind the heat. In fact, she felt like it softened her, released her tense muscles, thawed her soul.

It also made for the perfect excuse to wear her favorite pink sundress to dinner with Hallie and Wesley later that evening. They were celebrating big news. Hallie had called a few days earlier, bursting with excitement for Olivia to be the first one to know.

"Violet wants me to be her producer!" exclaimed Hallie. "I set up a meeting with her about it and she thinks I'm ready!" Olivia could hear Hallie smiling. Pride filled her chest.

"Hallie, that's awesome!" cheered Olivia. She had been getting ready for a meeting of her own. She pinned the phone to her ear and grabbed the blazer off her bed. "You deserve it! I'm so proud of you," she praised, locating her leather covered portfolio and placing it beside her black heels in her tote bag. She moved to her mirror and adjusted her dress. "Is that Wesley I hear in the background?"

Hallie laughed. "Yeah, he says 'hi.' We're just getting coffee. You know, carrying on the tradition in your honor."

"Aw, I miss you both," Olivia confessed. She turned off her bedroom lamp and walked to her door, bag in hand. "Let's get dinner this weekend to celebrate! How's Saturday?"

Hallie had agreed.

Olivia smiled as she thought back to their conversation. A bead of sweat dripped down her back as she continued down Third. She was glad Hallie had spoken up and been rewarded. Olivia had news of her own to share at dinner, too.

The day Hallie called her, Olivia had gone to a third-round interview with Golden Hour Productions, an unscripted production company, to work in its development department. She loved the possibility her next job would have her creating new ideas for TV shows. Ones hopefully more authentic than *Gator Guy*.

"I think your creativity and imagination would be great for a job like that," her mom encouraged over the phone. Olivia smiled, appreciating her support.

It had been nearly two months of temp jobs and interviews since her return from London. Olivia didn't mind the temp work; the woman who managed her was kind, and

Olivia found that tasks done without severe pressure were manageable, sometimes even enjoyable. It left her with time to run, tan in the park with Jess, and even consider cooking dinner before buying the same salad from Trader Joe's each night. Still, she was looking forward to something more permanent.

The interview had ended with the VP of the department, Linda, telling Olivia to "expect a call next week," with an obvious wink. Linda smiled and reached over to shake Olivia's hand from behind her desk. Olivia noticed it was adorned with photos of her son, her dog, and her partner. Linda's office walls held movie posters, wedding photos, a jersey autographed by Cristiano Ronaldo. There was even a large framed promo of the *Summer Season* cast, one of the many shows Golden Hour produced. Olivia caught Brad Bradley giving her a thumbs-up as she left Linda's office. The rest of the staff appeared to buzz with friendly conversation, the hours were normal, and while the pay wasn't substantial, it was definitely better than Atlas.

Olivia's strappy sandals continued down the block as she pictured her soon-to-be new job. She was excited to hear from Linda and hoped they'd speak first thing Monday morning. As Olivia neared the street corner, she found herself in front of a coffee shop.

The oversized door handle felt familiar in her hand. Plush chairs and metal stools filled the small interior. It was as if she could see Scott sitting in the middle of the shop.

Actually, she *did* see Scott.

He was typing on his laptop just left of the coffee bar, alone. She blinked her eyes several times. It was definitely him. She wondered where Other Olivia was.

While deciding if she could back out of the shop unnoticed, Scott's green eyes flicked up. He gave a small wave and stood up, collecting his laptop before walking over to greet Olivia by the door. She couldn't help but laugh, it was *so* like Scott to take something like the coffee shop she'd shown him and make it his.

"Hey stranger." He ran his hand through his hair and leaned against the wall. She was surprised by his eagerness to converse.

"What a coincidence to see you here," Olivia said casually. She tucked her hair behind her ear.

"Yeah, it's a chill place," he replied. "I had some work to do so I came by." He gestured to the backpack in his hand.

Olivia nodded. In the months she'd spent with Scott, she'd never known him to work on the weekends. Maybe he was starting to take his job more seriously. Set goals and work toward them. A sign of growth, maturation.

"Hey, so," Scott started. He smiled, shifting his weight and taking a step closer to her. She could smell his cologne, see the freckles on his face. She wondered again where Other Olivia could be.

"I know things have been weird between us," he continued, looking bashful while he rubbed a hand over his jaw. Her heartbeat quickened, she felt herself holding her breath. Had he finally realized how hard it was to balance a career and a love life? *Sweet redemption.*

She leaned closer, certain she was about to hear a heartfelt apology. An outpour of sorrow for how he'd ended things. Maybe he would cry!

"But," Scott cleared his throat, "I heard Kanye is in town this weekend." He gave a sheepish smile. "Any chance you have tickets?"

Olivia chuckled and took a step back. There was so much that had changed over the past eight months. But the green eyes, ash brown hair, and chiseled jaw in front of her had not changed at all.

It was so obvious to her now how hard she had been trying in all the wrong places. Olivia stared into Scott's eyes. The charm, the allure, it was still there, but now she knew: it would lead her nowhere.

"Actually," she answered honestly, "I don't work at Atlas anymore." It felt freeing to say out loud. She watched Scott's eyebrows raise in surprise.

"Wow, for real? You were like, Miss TV."

She nodded her head and gave a small smile. "Some things just don't work out. I think it's for the better."

He looked puzzled as she sidestepped around him, clearing his path toward the door.

"Good luck though, Scott," she finished.

He slung his backpack over his shoulder. "Bummer." He frowned. "Well, see you around."

Olivia didn't turn to watch him leave.

Instead she ordered an iced tea and sipped the cool drink as she leisurely walked to SoHo, popping into vintage shops, sampling soaps from expensive stores, and eventually meeting up with Hallie and Wesley.

"Raise a glass, cuz we kick ass!" mocked Hallie with a laugh as they clinked their drinks. They toasted to Hallie's promotion, to Olivia's hopeful new job, to Wesley's segment making it into Friday Wrap-Ups. Olivia couldn't stop smiling. She felt like she could be her true self around them.

She fell asleep that night grateful *Happy Hour* had left her with not one but two positive outcomes.

~

On Monday evening, Olivia walked home from her temp job in Union Square. It was a short distance from her apartment, but the light breeze through the heat was so inviting she found herself on the edge of Washington Square Park near West Fourth Street. She sat on a bench near the large fountain, watching small children dip their feet in the water, some braver ones even wading across. She remembered the time she and Gwen had thrown pennies into the gushing water, making a wish for the future ahead—she was almost certain her wish had been to be more like Violet.

Olivia fished in her bag for her phone, hoping she could catch Gwen and Henry before it grew too late in London. She looked at the screen and noticed a missed call from an unknown number. Cursing herself, she opened up her voicemail, eager to hear Linda from Golden Hour's voice. She brought the phone to her ear.

"Hi Olivia, this is James from the Hollywood Writers' Fellowship." She was startled to hear a man's voice. "I received your pilot script and application to our program. I was very impressed by your work and would like to invite you to join our Young Writers' Room in Los Angeles. Please give me a call back at your earliest convenience."

She rewound the message and played it again. And again.

The phone slipped from her hand onto the metal bench. She stared at it in shock.

She closed her eyes and tried to picture herself in LA. She *did* look good with a tan. Was she ready to leave New York City? Did she have what it took to follow another dream?

Olivia reached for her phone.

There was nothing ahead but endless possibilities.

ACKNOWLEDGMENTS

Thank you to Eric Koester and the entire Creator Institute for the opportunity to write this book. I'm forever grateful for your willingness to give me an outlet for my creative energy. I'd also like to thank my editors, Illia Epifanov and Bailee Noella; you read my chapters when they were mush and for that you should get an award. A special thank you to Haley Newlin and Emily VanderBent for your early coaching and encouragement. And thank you to the entire team at New Degree Press for working so hard to make this book possible.

To Chloe Cullen, thank you for planting this idea in my head and so expertly leading the way.

To my parents, thank you for your equal parts unwavering support and brutal honesty. This book would be only half as good without both of those qualities.

To my sister, I'm sorry that when I decided to write this book, it meant you by extension did too. Thank you for patiently reading every chapter alongside me.

To my grandmom, thank you for your constant praise and repeatedly telling me I'll be the "famous one" in the family.

To my entire extended family, you are all far more successful than I am, but it's clear Grandmom loves me best. Deal with it.

To my Beta Readers: Stephanie Dexter, Chloe Cullen, Kelsey Barberio, Daniela Tijerina, Carly Belsito, and Brandon Berman, I couldn't ask for better, more thoughtful people to trust with my first draft. Special thank you to Brandon for the title of this book.

To my amazing friends, thank you for not abandoning me when I consistently skipped happy hour. Somehow you always knew when and when *not* to ask how the book was going—that's true friendship.

To my Author Community and everyone who purchased my book during my presale campaign, I was blown away by your quick and eager support. You guys are the coolest and none of this would be possible without you. Special shout out to my first buyer, Susan Maffei, and to Kara McCarthy for coining the phrase "Boyfriend Island."

The following people went above and beyond in their presale support, thank you so much: Jillian Grzywacz, Maria Liberopoulos, David & Debbie Dexter, Stephanie Dexter, Jamie Edwards, The Daum family, Samantha & Christopher Atanacio, Sharon Perrone, Kate & Danny LaChance, Ginny and Robert Perrone, Susan Maffei, Jamie Hoover, The Matheson Family, Margaret Bajer, The Stein Family, Kathy and David Nebhut, Jennifer Boardman, Linda Ong, and Jimmy Knowles & Civic Entertainment Group.

And lastly, to *my* industry friends, I really don't know what I would do without you.

Made in the USA
Middletown, DE
07 July 2022

68734095R00116